D0016443

FOLK TOYS AROUND THE WORLD

AND HOW TO MAKE THEM

By Joan Joseph
Illustrated by Mel Furukawa

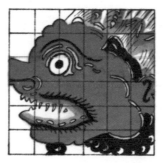

Working Drawings and Instructions
by Glenn Wagner

PARENTS' MAGAZINE PRESS
NEW YORK
In cooperation with the U.S. Committee for UNICEF

To Dr. Zelda S. Wolpe
who appreciates the dignity of all children

Text copyright © 1972 by Joan Joseph
Illustrations copyright © 1972 by Parents' Magazine Press
Printed in the United States of America
All rights reserved

Library of Congress Cataloging in Publication Data
Joseph, Joan.
     Folk toys around the world and how to make them.
     SUMMARY: Introduces eighteen toys from various
countries, gives directions for constructing them, and
discusses the materials needed.
     1. Toy making—Juvenile literature. [1. Toy making]
I. Furukawa, Mel, illus. II. Title.
TT174.J67   745.59'2   72-1127
ISBN 0-8193-0598-7 ISBN 0-8193-0599-5 (lib. bdg.)

CONTENTS

ACKNOWLEDGMENTS

I am greatly indebted to Dr. Subas Dhar, Inter Regional Advisor, Development Planning Advisory Services of the United Nations, who encouraged me in my concept of a book about toys in which young people around the world would learn a little of the national customs and histories not to be found in the usual history books. I wish to thank Mr. Jack Ling, Chief of the Public Information Division, UNICEF (United Nations Children's Fund), United Nations, New York, for introducing me to the United States Committee for UNICEF, which assisted me in further research.

I must warmly thank Mrs. Marie Walden, Department of Foreign Affairs, Helsinki, Finland; Mr. I. Davidovitch, Curator of the Museum of Ethnography, Ramat Aviv, Israel; the staff of the Museum of the Athens Institute of Folkloric Studies; the Islamic Institute of New York; as well as the many others who have assisted me in collecting folk toys from around the world.

I wish to express my deep gratitude to Betty Jordan Gluckman for her encouragement and understanding, and to Mr. Bert Cigge for his invaluable assistance.

My sincerest appreciation to the Yugoslavian children of the Vasa Carapić and Milovan Glišić elementary schools for the toys they so generously gave me; and a special note of thanks to many other boys and girls around the world, especially Peter Jordan and Robert Levy.

Last, but far from least, I wish to thank Dena Joseph for her untiring assistance in helping prepare this manuscript for press.

INTRODUCTION

ABOUT MATERIALS:

Most of the toys in this book can be made with inexpensive or scrap-size materials. A list of materials needed is given for each toy. Dimensions for the wood parts as well as other materials are given in finished sizes, except for a few cases where sufficient material is allowed for carving or shaping. Where native woods or materials were used on the original toy and may be unobtainable locally, adequate substitutes have been indicated where they will serve as well. Four of the toys have been either redesigned or adapted so that common materials can be used in their construction. Some sources of supply for thin, straight-grained basswood used in several of the toys are wooden yardsticks, paint paddles, and wooden Venetian blind slats. Basswood, sugar pine and white pine are suggested woods to use because they are easy to work and take fine finishes. Medium or hard balsa is a good substitute.

Two types of glue will be helpful in assembling the toys. First, a type called "white glue" is useful for bonding wood to wood and cloth to wood. There are several brands of this type. The second type, Duco household cement, will not only bond wood to wood, but metal to wood. Both types of glue dry clear and transparent.

One caution: Duco cement contains solvents that can ruin a table finish, so use suitable covering or, better yet, utilize a workbench.

ABOUT THE DRAWINGS:

For each toy there are two types of drawings—an artist's pictorial rendering which gives general construction details and suggested painting schemes—and full-size patterns and assembly detail working drawings from which direct measurements can be taken. A few drawings, because of the size of the toy and page size limitations, contain broken outlines, but are fully dimensioned where needed.

CONSTRUCTION AND TOOLS:

Since even the finest craftsmen may use different tools for different processes and make the parts of a toy in a different sequence, specific instructions on the selections and use of tools have not been given for each toy. However, tools which will do the work and, in a few instances, suggestions on how to do the operation have been given. The sequence of operations has been outlined so that the toy can be made easily and quickly. The following list contains tools which are *ideal* for making all the toys in the book. Some are commonly found in the home; others are not so easily available. Substitutions, however, can often be made, especially in the case of expensive tools such as the power jig saw or electric drill.

Claw hammer and ball-peen hammer.

A handsaw with crosscut teeth for roughing out stock.

A dovetail saw and/or a razor saw for fine work.

A coping saw and V-block or a power jig saw for cutting curves as well as fine cutting.

Hand drill and a set of drills from $1/16''$ to $1/4''$ by 32nds, and/or a $1/4''$ electric drill.

Brace and bits for boring holes larger than $1/4''$, $1/2''$ and $13/16''$ bits.

Hacksaw for cutting metal or bone.

Tin snips for cutting tin and cardboard.

Tweezers.

Pliers—round nose for bending round loops in wire—long nose for general assembly—electrician's for cutting and bending wire.

Chip carving or linoleum block cutting tools for carving wood.

A utility knife, modeler's knife with replaceable blades, and a jack-knife with large and small blades for general cutting and carving.

A sharpening stone and fish oil to keep tools sharp.

Small bench vise and c-clamps for holding material while working on it and clamping while glue dries. Also useful for clamping are spring clothespins and rubber bands.

6

A sharp pencil, ruler, and compass.

A try-square or combination square for layout work and checking squareness of material or assembly.

Wood rasp and fine-tooth mill file for roughing to size and finishing materials.

2/0, 3/0, and 6/0 garnet finishing paper for sanding and finishing.

ABOUT FINISHES:

Shellac may be used for a sealer on all wood parts that require a painted finish. Vinyl sealer is excellent also. Allow sealers to dry thoroughly, preferably overnight, before painting toys.

Paints made for model railroad equipment, model airplanes, and model cars are ideal for finishing most toys. They are available at hobby shops in small quantities in a variety of colors. Most may be applied to wood without a primer, on metal after a metal primer has been applied. Model railroad colors usually are flat paints; model airplane and car paints are glossy. Buy a bottle of thinner to match the paints you use for cleaning brushes. Use good artist's sable brushes for a fine finish.

FIVE DOLLS FROM YUGOSLAVIA

Imagine going to school where "toy making" is a compulsory subject. It is possible. In Yugoslavia all children in grades one to four are taught the fun and creativity of making their own playthings. By the time they are in grade five, they have graduated from simple toy making and begun receiving instruction in the traditional folk arts of their country.

Steeped in centuries of tradition, the Yugoslavians are not willing to allow the industrialization and mass production of the 20th century to sweep away the artistic creativity of their exquisite handicrafts. The folk art of Yugoslavia is an integral part of the cultural heritage of the people, and today—more than ever before—Yugoslavians are determined that the beauties of their past must not only be preserved, but allowed to blend with the technological achievements of modern times.

Here are five dolls that you can put on your desk or bookshelf, or give as presents.

PESTLE DOLL

MATERIALS:

1 pc. 2" square x 5½" basswood, pine, or balsa for the body; assorted colors of thin leather in small sizes for the skirt, arms, hands, headband, toothpick pouch and pouch bottom as per drawings; ⅛" x 3" strip of fine gray fur for the hat; ¼" x 2" strip of black fur or felt for the hair; blue, red, white, green, brown and black model paints; Duco-type household cement, or white glue.

HOW TO MAKE IT:

1. Turn on a wood lathe, or carve by hand, the body and head in one piece. Sand smooth. Drill a $\frac{3}{16}$" hole through the body for the arms.

2. Shellac the wood, or use a vinyl sealer. Allow to dry.

3. Make all the leather parts. Cut fringe as indicated on drawings.

4. Paint the body brown between the neck and skirt lines, then paint the dress design on the front.

5. Paint the eyes and eyebrows. Allow paint to dry.

6. Glue the skirt around the base.

7. Slip the arm thong through the arm hole in the body, then glue on the hands. Glue hands to the skirt also.

8. Glue the fur strip across the head from side to side.

9. Glue the hair in place in front of the fur strip.

10. Glue the headband on top of the hair, just in front of the fur strip.

11. Make the toothpick pouch by rolling the leather around a piece of $\frac{1}{2}$" wood dowel; apply glue where the leather overlaps. Cover the dowel first with waxed paper to prevent glue from sticking to the dowel. Glue the bottom disc to the tube thus formed. Remove pouch from dowel after glue is dry. Glue pouch on front of the doll.

NEWSPAPER BOY

MATERIALS:

1–2" and 2–8¼" lengths of #14 copper wire for the body frame (use house-wiring cable; remove the insulation); #18 bell wire, plastic insulated, blue and white, for the arm, body, and leg wrapping; 1–$\frac{11}{16}$" diameter wood bead for the head; small scraps of black and white felt for the cap and visor; newspaper clippings and green card stock for the miniature newspapers; Duco-type household cement, or white glue; red and black model paint; gold embroidery thread.

HOW TO MAKE IT:

1. Bend the two 8¼" lengths of #14 copper wire into arm, body, and leg contours using the full size drawing as a guide.

2. Lay the three pieces of wire flat on a smooth surface with waxed paper underneath, then apply Duco-type cement where the three wires meet to form the body. Allow cement to dry.

3. Wrap the legs and body portion of the pants with the blue plastic-insulated bell wire. Make coils tight and smooth.

4. Wrap torso and arm sections as per drawing with the white plastic-insulated wire in the same manner.

5. Now bend the feet outward and the arms downward with hands forward in a realistic pose. See that the boy stands firmly on his feet.

6. Glue the wood bead on the end of the neck wire. Allow glue to dry.

7. Paint the eyes, eyebrows, nose nostril dots and hair black, the mouth red.

8. Cut out the cap and visor parts from felt. Glue the two black pieces together first, then add the white visor.

9. Glue the cap on the head in a rakish position.

10. Fold four layers of newspaper and four of green card stock together to make the miniature "newspapers." Punch holes for the boy's wire loop hands. Tie several strands of gold embroidery floss to the green newspaper to make a neck strap.

11. Slip the small newspaper pack over the right hand wire loop. Hang the gold floss around the boy's neck and slip the green newspaper bundle under his left hand loop.

WOODEN SPOON DOLLS

MATERIALS:

1 wooden spoon; bits of colored cloth, braid, felt, fur, sequins; Duco-type cement, or white glue.

HOW TO MAKE THEM:

1. The size and proportion of the dolls will depend upon spoon size.

2. Paint a face in the bowl of the spoon—or on the back.

3. Use felt or fur for hair.

4. Cover the handle with pieces of colored cloth, braid, or felt in any

NEWSPAPER BOY

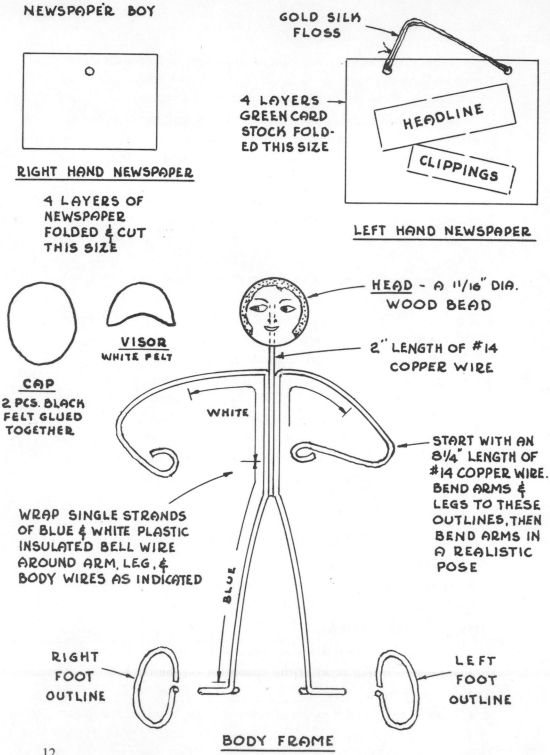

RIGHT HAND NEWSPAPER

4 LAYERS OF
NEWSPAPER
FOLDED & CUT
THIS SIZE

GOLD SILK
FLOSS

4 LAYERS
GREEN CARD
STOCK FOLD-
ED THIS SIZE

HEADLINE

CLIPPINGS

LEFT HAND NEWSPAPER

CAP
2 PCS. BLACK
FELT GLUED
TOGETHER

VISOR
WHITE FELT

HEAD - A 11/16" DIA.
WOOD BEAD

2" LENGTH OF #14
COPPER WIRE

WHITE

START WITH AN
8¼" LENGTH OF
#14 COPPER WIRE.
BEND ARMS &
LEGS TO THESE
OUTLINES, THEN
BEND ARMS IN
A REALISTIC
POSE

WRAP SINGLE STRANDS
OF BLUE & WHITE PLASTIC
INSULATED BELL WIRE
AROUND ARM, LEG, &
BODY WIRES AS INDICATED

BLUE

**RIGHT
FOOT
OUTLINE**

**LEFT
FOOT
OUTLINE**

BODY FRAME

12

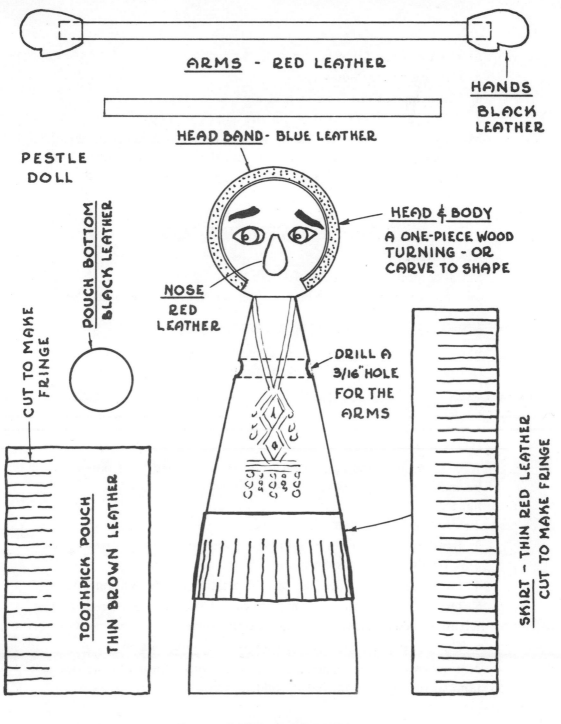

ARMS - RED LEATHER

HANDS
BLACK
LEATHER

HEAD BAND - BLUE LEATHER

PESTLE
DOLL

POUCH BOTTOM
BLACK LEATHER

HEAD & BODY

A ONE-PIECE WOOD
TURNING - OR
CARVE TO SHAPE

NOSE
RED
LEATHER

DRILL A
3/16" HOLE
FOR THE
ARMS

CUT TO MAKE FRINGE

TOOTHPICK POUCH
THIN BROWN LEATHER

SKIRT - THIN RED LEATHER
CUT TO MAKE FRINGE

FULL SIZE PATTERNS
& DETAILS

13

design you wish. Glue materials to the handle.

5. Use sequins for buttons.

6. Use scraps of felt for ears and nose.

7. A square of cloth folded diagonally will make a lady's head shawl. Make it large enough so the shawl can be fitted around the head realistically. Tie a colored string around the neck to hold the loose ends secure on the front side.

MARTIAN MEDICINE MAN

MATERIALS:

Small cardboard boxes, or boxes cut down to size, for the body. Pill and medicine boxes are ideal. Suggested sizes for the parts: head 1½″ x 2″ x 2″, neck 1″ x 1″ x 1½″, body 1½″ x 2½″ x 5″, legs 1″ x 1″ x 4½″, arms ½″ x ½″ x 3½″, feet 1½″ x 1½″ x 2″, #18 bell wire, plastic insulated, assorted colors, for nose, ears, and antennae; bits of colored plastic tape or felt for eyes and mouth; colored paper for the hands; Duco-type household cement, or white glue; assorted model paints (optional).

HOW TO MAKE IT:

1. Collect the boxes before construction begins. Any size boxes can be used, but keep the various sizes in proportion to make a good figure.

2. Glue boxes together.

3. Bend insulated bell wire into spirals for ears and nose. Antennae may be straight pieces or spiraled. Glue wire to boxes.

4. Paint the boxes if desired, or add plastic tape decorations.

5. Draw the eyes, nose and mouth, or cut pieces of plastic tape or felt to represent these details and apply to face.

6. Cut out paper hands—see artist's sketch—glue to arms.

Note: Arms may be fastened to the body with adhesive or masking tape so they can be moved up and down.

CARDBOARD TUBE DOLLS

MATERIALS:

Cardboard tubes from bathroom tissue or paper towels, or small mailing tubes; bits of cloth, braid, used postage stamps, newspaper clippings, old nylon stockings, knitting yarn for decorations; Duco-type household cement, or white glue.

HOW TO MAKE THEM:

1. Cover the cardboard tube with colored paper; glue to tube at the seam.

2. Cover the top of the tube. Make a hat or cap.

3. Draw face details, or make nose and ears of felt.

4. Decorate any way you choose.

YO-YO FROM
THE PHILIPPINE ISLANDS—
GREECE

W ho invented the yo-yo? Where is it from? Its modern name was coined by the late Donald Franklin Duncan in 1932, but its history is tied to those legendary pages before recorded time; there alone lies the answer to the origins of this curious little toy.

In the days of the pharaohs, 3000–2000 B.C., Egyptian children are known to have played with this fascinating toy and it was also known in the Far East in ancient times, but its country of origin remains a mystery. Furthermore, as obscure as is its history, so is it difficult to imagine the little yo-yo as a deadly weapon; yet it is even conceivable that it was originally invented for this purpose.

Regardless of its origin, the yo-yo unquestionably forms a part of the early history of Filipino weaponry. Among the peoples of the Philippine Islands, stories have come down from generation to generation of how in the "olden days" one of the most effective weapons was the yo-yo. It is said that the attacker would hide among the highest branches of a tree, wait patiently for his enemy to pass below, and then skillfully release his yo-yo, striking his victim on the head. The forceful, well-directed blow was almost always fatal.

During the Dark Ages in Europe, the yo-yo was dormant; it stayed out of sight until the 1790's when it was brought to France by missionaries from the Court of Peking. The hitherto "sleeping yo-yo" began to gain momentum with such speed that the émigrette—the new little

settler—as it was called, spread across France and became the craze of children throughout the country.

Then, for some unknown reason, its popularity waned and for over one hundred years it was nowhere to be seen. Suddenly, in the 1920's, the yo-yo returned. The fun of yo-yoing swept across England and America; children and adults were mesmerized by the little weight running up and down a string. Around the world it traveled:

17

in France it was now called a Bandelure, or winding toy; in England, a Prince-of-Wales' toy; and all Europe knew the name Quiz.

The Persians condemned it—but to no avail: "This game," a Persian newspaper wrote, "like the deadly plagues which used to come from India or Arabia, has come from Europe . . . even mothers who formerly attended to the care of children and households, now spend their time playing yo-yo."

The yo-yos of children in the hamlets of modern Greece are easy to make, and soon you, too, can be yo-yoing as they do.

MATERIALS:

2 or 4—1½" to 2" diameter flat coat buttons—the larger the buttons, the easier they will be to hold—the heavier the buttons the easier to yo-yo; 1—2½" length of #18 copper or soft iron wire—or straighten out two sides of a 1" long paper clip; 1—7' length of fine cord—use heavy fishing line, builder's cord, or yo-yo string.

HOW TO MAKE IT:

1. Align the buttons back-to-back. If you use four buttons, sew one button of each pair together first with fine thread.
2. Bend the wire into a U-shape, then push the ends through the buttonholes.
3. Twist the ends of the wire together, using pliers. To keep the inside buttons parallel and about ¼" apart while tightening the wire, slip several thicknesses of cardboard about 1½" square between the buttons to act as spacers. Cut notches in the cardboard to clear the wire.
4. Cut off excess length of the wire close to the button with wire cutters or electrician's pliers. Bend the remaining twisted portion flat against the center recess in the button.
5. Holding the buttons with the fingers of both hands, twist one set of buttons one to two turns to twist the wires together at the center.
6. Remove cardboard spacers.
7. Tie one end of the cord to the center of the yo-yo. Tie a two-inch finger loop in the other end.

TO USE YOUR YO-YO:

Wind up the cord between the buttons. Slip the finger loop over the third finger of either hand; hold the yo-yo between your thumb and third finger. Now let the yo-yo drop from your fingers. The momentum of its spinning as it drops will rewind the cord when the yo-yo reaches the end of it and return the yo-yo to your hand. After working it up and down a few times, try spinning it at an angle, then horizontally, then vertically again. Soon you'll be able to perform many gymnastics with it. Make two yo-yos and try spinning one in each hand for more fun.

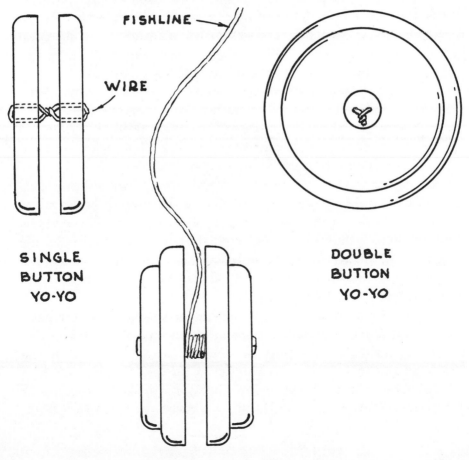

FISHLINE

WIRE

SINGLE
BUTTON
YO-YO

DOUBLE
BUTTON
YO-YO

THE THUNDERBOLT FROM
NEW ZEALAND AND
BULL-ROARER FROM NEW MEXICO

Around the world, the eerie sounds of the bull-roarer have attracted attention for centuries. Originally, the bull-roarer was a religious and magical object. It was known in ancient times in central Africa as well as by the Indians of pre-Columbian America. It was used by the peoples of Tibet and the Eskimos of Canada.

In New Zealand, the *Tohunga*—one of the priestly group of the Maori people—called the bull-roarer a *Purerehua,* or Thunderbolt. The Tohungas whirled it to frighten away the evil spirits that helped the God of Storms; and conversely, in times of drought, swung it round and round to summon the God of Rain.

In ancient Greece, the bull-roarer was often whirled during performances of the sacred mysteries, and in the southwestern United States, the noise of the Indians' sacred lightning stick was symbolic of the sound of thunder. The ceremonial significance of the lightning stick is still maintained by these Indians, as is the tradition that the stick will be endowed with magical powers only if it has been made from a tree struck by lightning.

The sacred significance of the bull-roarer lessened with the passing of time, and it became a popular toy around the world.

Today, in the 20th century, whether it is called a Wolf by the children of Czechoslovakia, a Monster by those of New Caledonia, a Howler by children living in the southern Appalachian region of America; or elsewhere as a Hummer, a Swish, or a Thunder Stick,

this wonderful noisemaker continues to maintain its appeal for children.

THUNDERBOLT

MATERIALS:

1 pc. ¼″ x 2½″ x 6″ pine or basswood for the blade; 1—27″ length of heavy twine such as builder's chalk line; 1—½″ x 7″ wood dowel for the handle.

HOW TO MAKE IT:

1. Make a pattern for the oval shape of the blade by folding a 2½″ x 6″ piece of paper in two lengthwise; then sketch one-half the outline. Cut with scissors. Trace the pattern on the wood. Cut out the ellipse using a coping saw or power jig saw.

2. Locate the hole center, then drill a ⅛″ hole for the cord. Countersink the hole on both sides.

3. Sand edges and surfaces smooth; round all corners.

4. Apply a coat of shellac or vinyl sealer; allow to dry.

5. Sketch and paint the design, or carve the design into the wood as New Zealanders do.

6. Fasten one end of the cord to the blade, the other end to the hole drilled in the top of the handle as shown in the artist's sketch.

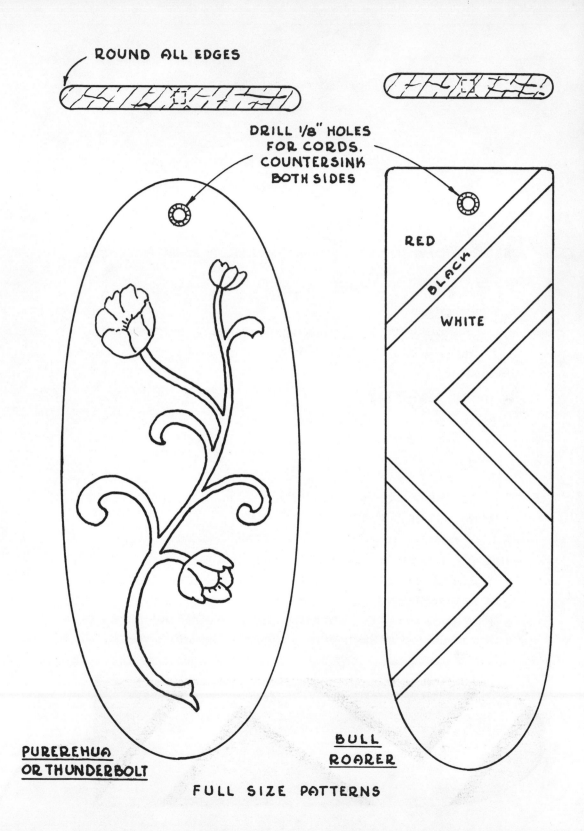

ROUND ALL EDGES

DRILL 1/8" HOLES
FOR CORDS.
COUNTERSINK
BOTH SIDES

RED

BLACK

WHITE

PUREREHUA
OR THUNDERBOLT

BULL
ROARER

FULL SIZE PATTERNS

TO USE YOUR THUNDERBOLT:

Your thunderbolt must be used outdoors in a clear area. To prevent injury as the blade swings, see that no one is close by. Hold the handle in one hand, then swing the blade in a circle over your head, gradually increasing speed until your thunderbolt roars in the wind.

BULL ROARER

MATERIALS:

1 pc. ¼″ x 1¾″ x 6¼″ white pine or basswood for the blade; 1—4′ length of heavy twine such as builder's chalk line; shellac or vinyl sealer; red, white, and black model paints.

HOW TO MAKE IT:

1. Cut the blade to size. Locate and drill the ⅛″ hole for the cord. Countersink the hole on both sides.

2. Sketch the pointed end outline, then cut to shape with a coping saw or power jig saw. Round all edges with a wood rasp or coarse sandpaper wrapped around a block of wood.

3. Finish sanding with 2/0, then 3/0 paper.

4. Apply a coat of shellac or vinyl wood sealer; allow to dry. Then sand lightly with 6/0 finishing paper.

5. Paint suggested design or one of your own.

6. Attach one end of the cord to the blade with a bowline or similar knot. Tie a two-inch finger loop in the other end.

TO USE YOUR BULL-ROARER:

Your bull-roarer must be used outdoors in a clear area. To prevent injury as the blade swings, see that no one is close by. Slip the finger loop in the cord over your first two fingers. Now swing your bull-roarer in a circle over your head, gradually increasing speed until it roars in the wind.

TUMBLING MAN
FROM AUSTRIA

The Chinese have invaded Vienna! This was the cry of Viennese toy merchants in the early years of the 19th century. The children of Austria were fascinated by the spectacular displays and explosive sounds created by Chinese fireworks; dominoes, a newly imported game, was not only the rage of the Austro-Hungarian Empire, but rapidly spread throughout Europe, becoming a popular pastime of children everywhere; hardly a toy store could be found that did not feature Chinese building-blocks and shadow puppets, and "made in China" became associated with toys children would unquestionably enjoy.

Austrian children were especially fond of the tumbling clown. His lifelike antics delighted young and old alike; they all were filled with laughter when the funny little jointed man tumbled head over heels down a flight of stairs, for he always landed in a most comical position. Few children understood that his acrobatic somersaults were caused by the sliding action of the quicksilver that had been placed in his papier-mâché head.

The clown, a familiar character since Greek and Roman times, was a natural subject for a children's toy. Audiences from every walk of life—kings and queens as well as peasants and serfs—had always been amused by the strange gesticulations and bodily contortions that he executed when called upon to give his pantomime performances. It was left to the Chinese to prove that the laughter of an audience, excited by a live clown, could be recaptured with a tumbling toy.

The success of the Chinese tumbler inspired Austrian toy makers to create a tumbling man of their own, a funny little character whose acrobatic tricks still evoke laughter from children and adults alike.

The modern tumbling clown is extremely simple to make. A small ball bearing has been substituted for quicksilver, and felt is used instead of wood.

MATERIALS:

Small pieces of colored felt as per patterns for the body, mittens, and cap; 1 pc. 1″ x 6″ cut from an index card for the head tube; 2 pcs. $\frac{1}{16}$″ thick x $\frac{3}{4}$″ diameter cardboard for the tube ends; 1–$\frac{1}{2}$″ diameter steel ball bearing (automobile wheel bearing—obtainable at a local garage) for the head weight; white glue.

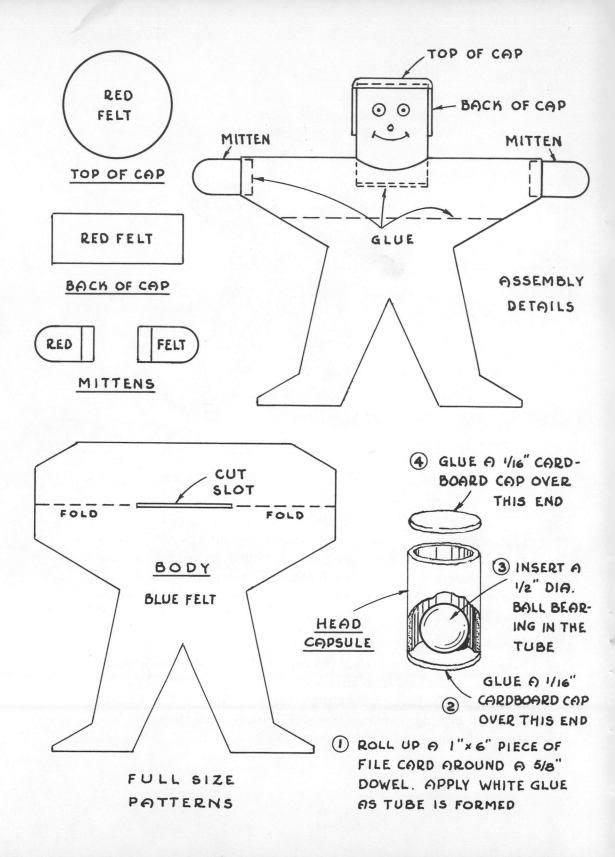

TOP OF CAP

RED
FELT

TOP OF CAP

RED FELT

BACK OF CAP

RED | FELT

MITTENS

TOP OF CAP

BACK OF CAP

MITTEN

MITTEN

GLUE

ASSEMBLY
DETAILS

CUT
SLOT

FOLD   FOLD

BODY

BLUE FELT

FULL SIZE
PATTERNS

④ GLUE A 1/16" CARD-
BOARD CAP OVER
THIS END

③ INSERT A
1/2" DIA.
BALL BEAR-
ING IN THE
TUBE

HEAD
CAPSULE

GLUE A 1/16"
CARDBOARD CAP
② OVER THIS END

① ROLL UP A 1"x 6" PIECE OF
FILE CARD AROUND A 5/8"
DOWEL. APPLY WHITE GLUE
AS TUBE IS FORMED

HOW TO MAKE IT:

1. Trace the drawings to make paper patterns for the body, mittens, and cap. Cut the parts from colored felt.

2. Make the head next. Roll the 1″ x 6″ piece of index card around a ⅝″ wood dowel to form the head tube, applying a thin film of white glue after the paper overlaps. Wrap a rubber band around the tube to hold it in shape until the glue dries. Remove the tube from the dowel.

3. Glue a piece of 1/16″ thick cardboard over each end of the tube after the ball bearing has been inserted. Wait until glue dries. Trim flush with the outside of the tube after glue is dry.

4. Glue the felt cap disc over one end of the head tube, molding the overlapping edges down over the sides to form the top of the cap. Then glue the cap back around the tube under this piece, centering it over the seam of the tube.

5. Draw face details with a pen, or use colored pencils.

6. Cut the slot in the body. Fold felt over; glue mittens in place.

7. Glue head in body slot.

TO USE YOUR TUMBLING MAN:

Place him on a board held at an angle, then watch him tumble head-over-heels as the ball bearing rolls from one end of the tube to the other.

A TWIRLING YO-YO
FROM THE WEST INDIES

This 4000-year-old toy is a challenge to any creative imagination. It is a string toy which, like the yo-yo, works on the principle of momentum. In this case, however, the momentum is created by forcefully pulling the string outward and then releasing it to rewind on its own.

It is one of the most popular handmade toys in the West Indies where it is made with four shiny bean pods called "cacoons." In the south of India this "twirling toy," as it is called by Indian children, is carved from wood and resembles a spinning umbrella; whereas in Czechoslovakia the same basic toy is created with a beautiful doll on a stand; she is known as the "Dancer from the Prahamy Heights," for if you pull the string, she gracefully twirls around her platform.

A most interesting version of this toy, dating as far back as the 20th century B.C., was found at the site of an Egyptian pyramid. Here archaeologists uncovered three ivory figures that looked like the Pygmies of central Africa; they named them "the dancing dwarfs." The little handcarved men stood on spoollike bases which were loosely fitted on a long ivory stand. It is believed that strings were fastened to the spools and run through the holes on the side of the stand. By twisting the figures to wind the thread, and then pulling the thread out rapidly, you could make the carved figures twirl.

As the centuries passed, these "dancing dwarfs"—the earliest known example of this string toy—traveled around the world, taking on the character of each country which adopted the principle of their movement and then laid claim to their creation as an original folk toy of its own culture.

From the 15th to the 18th century, the Applemill was a favorite plaything of English children, while the *Moulinet à Noix* delighted youngsters all over France. The modern Cacoon Yo-yo, as it is called in the West Indies, is almost identical to the Moulinet à Noix, differing only in the use of dried pods instead of nuts.

Since cacoon bean pods are unobtainable in temperate zones, this toy has been redesigned, using carved wood blocks to simulate bean pods. The bearing bean has been redesigned also so that it can be made of wood.

29

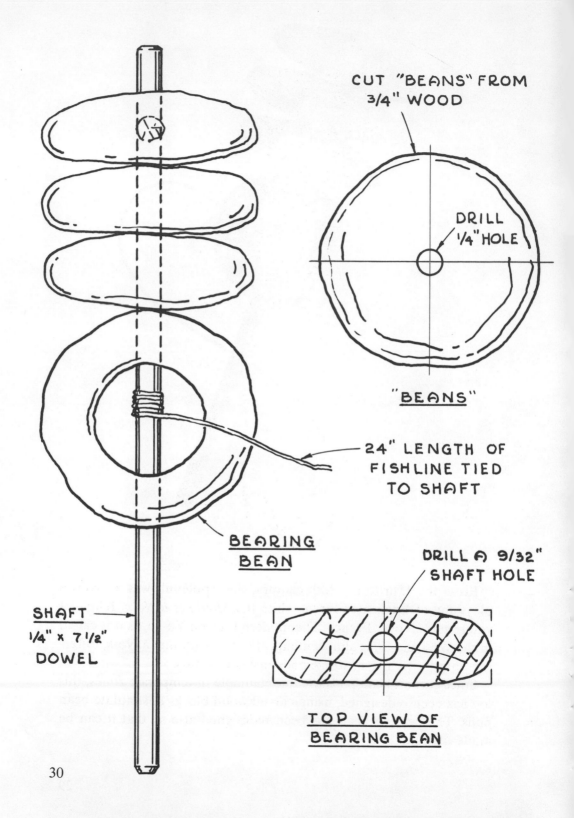

CUT "BEANS" FROM 3/4" WOOD

DRILL 1/4" HOLE

"BEANS"

24" LENGTH OF FISHLINE TIED TO SHAFT

BEARING BEAN

DRILL A 9/32" SHAFT HOLE

TOP VIEW OF BEARING BEAN

SHAFT 1/4" x 7 1/2" DOWEL

30

MATERIALS:

4—¾" x 2½" square wood blocks for the "beans"—use walnut or mahogany if available, or substitute pine or basswood; 1—¼" x 7½" wood dowel for the shaft; 30" length of fishline.

HOW TO MAKE IT:

1. Locate the centers on the sides of the wood blocks. Draw a 2¼" diameter circle on all the blocks, and an additional 1⅛" diameter circle on the bearing block. Locate the shaft hole center on one end of the bearing block.

2. Drill ¼" shaft holes through three of the blocks and a 9/32" hole vertically through the center of the bearing block.

3. Cut the outlines of the "beans" and the hole center in the bearing block for the string opening using a coping saw or power jig saw.

4. Rasp or carve the blocks to an elliptical shape resembling beans, then sand smooth.

5. Stain the blocks a chocolate brown to resemble the colors of the original toy beans.

6. Press the three horizontal beans on the shaft.

7. Slide the bearing bean in position under the three horizontal beans, then tie one end of the fishline tightly on the shaft so it won't slip. Tie a finger loop in the other end of the cord. The shaft should rotate freely in the bearing holes.

TO USE YOUR TWIRLING YO-YO:

Wind the fishline on the shaft by turning the shaft. Hold the bearing bean in one hand, then pull the cord evenly with the other, releasing tension as soon as the cord unwinds, allowing it to rewind itself on the shaft as the beans rotate. Repeat the operation, causing the beans to rotate first in one direction, then the other.

SPEAR-THE-FISH FROM
THE PRE-COLUMBIAN AMERICAS

From the snow-clad terrain of the Arctic wastelands to the bleak archipelago at the tip of South America, Eskimo and Indian tribes inhabited the Americas of pre-Columbian times. They were not a unified people, but were divided into many nations. Some roamed the Plains, like the Blackfoot of North America, and others, such as the Incas of South America, founded great empires. But even with greatly contrasting cultures and civilizations, there was a common heritage that was Indian. They were not the silent, somber savages stereotyped on movie and television screens, but rather a highly civilized, fun-loving people.

Hunting and spear fishing were an important part of the life of every Indian male, and the value of accurate marksmanship was impressed upon every Indian boy. Spear throwing and arrow shooting were an essential part of a boy's education, and innumerable games were invented to help youngsters gain these skills.

One of the most popular of these games was *Pommawonga—* Spear-the-fish. Its variations were endless; its name changed as the toy was altered and its construction was modified depending upon the natural materials at hand. The Eskimo, who used walrus ivory and an ivory pin, called the game *Gazinta;* the Iroquois played *Zimba* with conical-shaped bones and a stick; and in Ecuador the children still play Toss and Catch with a small barrelshaped block of wood and a wooden pin.

Whether it was called "Hoop and Pole," "Ring and Ping," or "Lovers' Game," the basic principle of Pommawonga was the same.

32

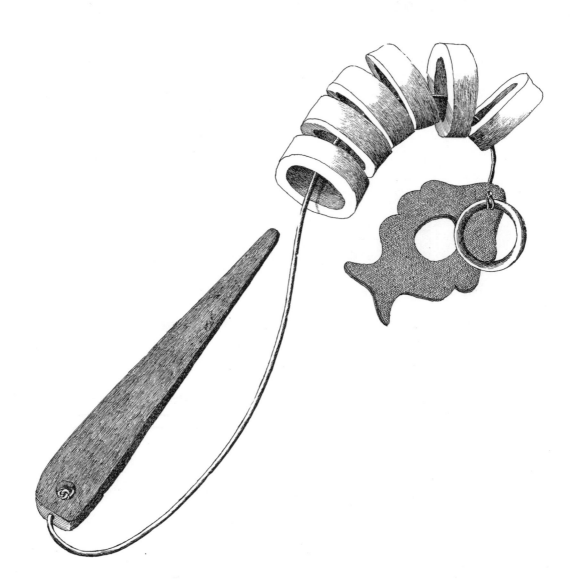

Regardless of how the toy was fashioned, this game of skill, so excellent for training the eye, was a favorite of Indian and Eskimo children throughout the Americas. Furthermore, its popularity was not confined to the youth of the two continents; the challenge of seeing how many bones could be caught on a pin intrigued even adults, who often gambled for stakes when they played the game.

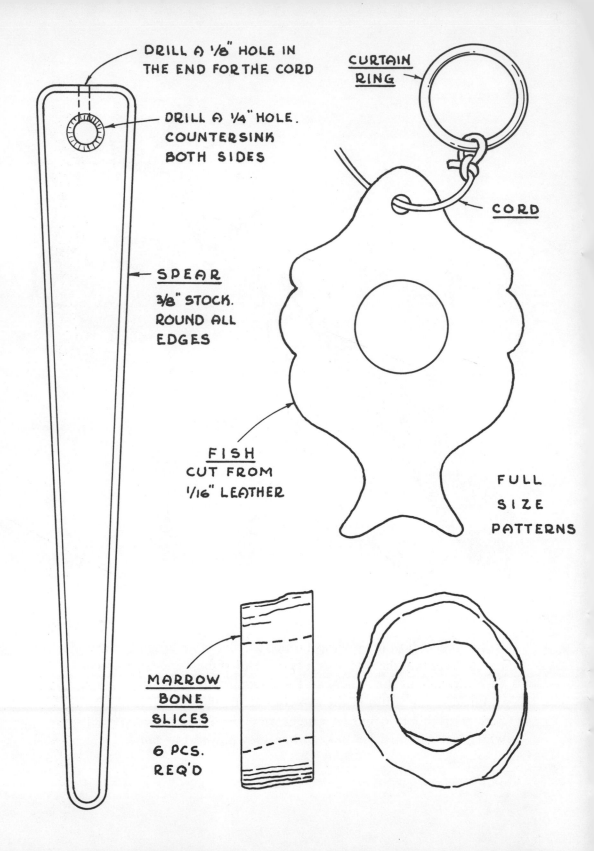

DRILL A 1/8" HOLE IN
THE END FOR THE CORD

DRILL A 1/4" HOLE.
COUNTERSINK
BOTH SIDES

CURTAIN
RING

CORD

SPEAR
3/8" STOCK.
ROUND ALL
EDGES

FISH
CUT FROM
1/16" LEATHER

FULL
SIZE
PATTERNS

MARROW
BONE
SLICES

6 PCS.
REQ'D

MATERIALS:

1 pc. ⅜" x 1" x 7½" pine, basswood, or any hardwood for the spear; 1 pc. 2½"x 4" leather ¹/₁₆"to ⅛" thick for the fish; 6 pcs. marrow bone cut about ¾" thick having center openings not less than 1" diameter; 1—1" diameter metal curtain ring; 1—24" length of builder's cord (chalk line) or heavy twine.

HOW TO MAKE IT:

1. Have the bones cut at a butcher shop if possible. Otherwise cut the bone slices with a hacksaw.

2. Boil the bones until they are clean. Allow them to dry thoroughly before use.

3. Make the spear. Locate centers and drill the ¼" and ⅛" holes first. Countersink the ¼" hole slightly on both sides. Then cut the tapers on both sides by planing or whittling. Round all edges with sandpaper, then sand wood until it is smooth.

4. Make a cardboard pattern for the fish and use it to cut the outline of the fish on the leather with a modeler's knife, or scissors.

5. Slip the leather fish on the cord, then tie one end of the cord to the curtain ring. Thread the other end through the hole in the end of the spear, tie a knot at the end, then pull cord taut to draw the cord into the ¼" hole so it will be centered in the spearhead.

TO USE YOUR SPEAR-THE-FISH:

Hold the leather fish, curtain ring and loose bones in one hand, the spear in the other. Now throw the bones, one at a time, into the air and try to catch them on the spear. When you catch a bone on the spear, thread it on the cord. Total number of bones caught is your score. You can score ten points for each bone caught if you prefer.

For a harder game, make six leather fish. Then alternate one bone and one fish as you toss them into the air. For scoring, the fish could count 100, each bone 10. Make up a scoring system of your own if you like. Take turns competing with your friends.

BALANCING FISHERMAN
FROM PORTUGAL

Since prehistoric times, man has been intrigued with the skill of balancing objects. And to this day, though scientists have long since mastered the mathematical laws of gravity, there is something fascinating about watching a balanced object lean and sway and yet not topple to the ground.

The balancing toy was a natural outgrowth of man's awareness of gravitational forces at work; and though Sir Isaac Newton of England is credited with having deduced the classic law of gravity, it would be impossible to give any one country the distinction of having invented the first balancing toy which certainly preceded his successful research.

Balancing toys, found in all parts of the world, reflect the culture and physical environment of their originators. In India balancing toys are carved in the shape of Hanuman, the Monkey God who is well known to Indian children, for he is their symbol of sportsmanship and fair play. And the woodcutter with his saw is certainly in keeping with the terrain of Finland, 71 percent of which is still covered with forests. In Portugal, where for centuries the people have earned their livelihood from the sea, the fisherman has been aptly chosen for a balancing toy.

There is no end to the shapes, forms and materials that can be used in making a balancing toy, as long as it is remembered that the weight of the figure to be balanced must be well below the center of gravity.

MATERIALS:

1 pc. ⅝″ square x 1¹³⁄₁₆″ pine or basswood for the body; 2—1½″-16 finishing nails for the legs; 1—¾″-17 wire nail for pants-to-body assembly; 1—2⅞″ length #18 wire for the arms; 1—15″ length #18 wire for the fishpole and line; 1—1⅛″ length ¹⁄₁₆″ diameter plastic tubing for the fishing pole; 1—1⅝″ length ³⁄₁₆″ diameter plastic tubing for the coatsleeves; 1—2¹⁄₁₆″ length ¼″ diameter plastic tubing for the pants; 1 pc. 1¼″ x 2¾″ tin can stock for the fish; assorted model paints.

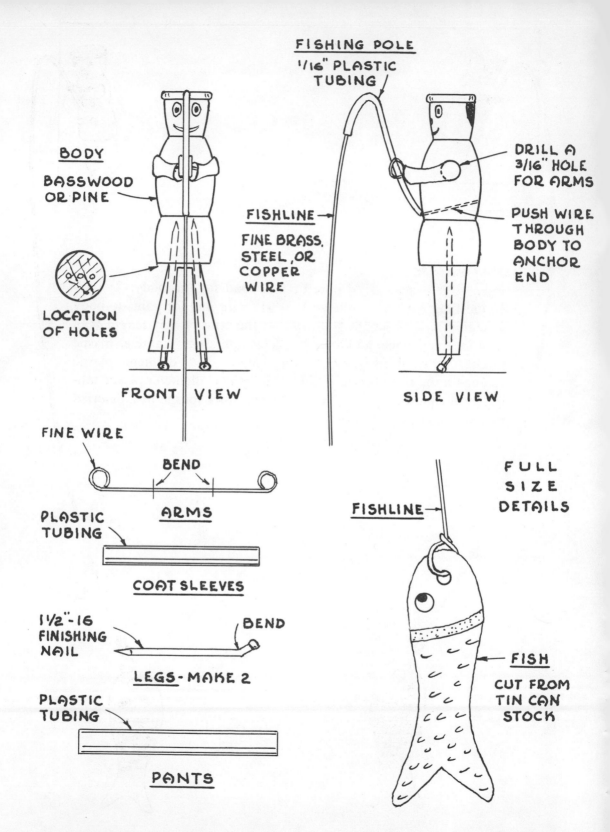

BODY

BASSWOOD OR PINE

LOCATION OF HOLES

FRONT VIEW

FISHING POLE
1/16" PLASTIC TUBING

FISHLINE

FINE BRASS, STEEL, OR COPPER WIRE

DRILL A 3/16" HOLE FOR ARMS

PUSH WIRE THROUGH BODY TO ANCHOR END

SIDE VIEW

FINE WIRE

BEND

ARMS

PLASTIC TUBING

COAT SLEEVES

1 1/2"-16 FINISHING NAIL

BEND

LEGS - MAKE 2

PLASTIC TUBING

PANTS

FISHLINE

FULL SIZE DETAILS

FISH

CUT FROM TIN CAN STOCK

HOW TO MAKE IT:

1. Carve or turn on a wood lathe the contours of the body. Use the full size drawing as a guide. Sand smooth. Paint the body blue, face flesh-color, cap red, hair black. Add eyes, nose, and mouth. (Note: the original toy body was a wood turning.)

2. Drill the $\frac{3}{16}''$ hole for the arms. Drill $\frac{1}{16}''$ pilot holes for the leg nails. See drawing detail.

3. Make and assemble the legs next. Press the $\frac{3}{4}''$-17 wire nail through the center of the pants tubing, then drive the nail into the center of the body block.

4. Bend the finishing nails slightly with pliers near the heads to form the feet, then press the nails into the pilot holes in the body block. Fold tubing as nails are inserted into holes to form pantslegs.

5. Form the loops in the ends of the arm wire, slip the coatsleeve tubing over the wire, insert the assembly into the arm hole in the body, then bend arms forward and together at the hands.

6. Cut the fish outline from the tin can stock with tin snips or shears. Drill a hole for the fishline wire. Paint the fish.

7. Form a bow in the fishline wire, then make a $\frac{1}{4}''$ loop in one end; hang the fish on the loop. Slip the $\frac{1}{16}''$ tubing over the other end of the wire, push the wire through the body from front to back to anchor it (see drawing), then bend to form the fishing pole.

TO USE YOUR BALANCING FISHERMAN:

Set him on the edge of a table with the fishline hanging free and watch him rock slightly as he fishes.

HAMAN KNOCKER
FROM ISRAEL

The story of Purim, as told in the Biblical Book of Esther, presents a vivid narrative of the persecution and deliverance of the Jewish people throughout the Persian Empire. Though it lacks historic authenticity, it has left an indelible imprint on the history of the Jewish people. "When all other festivals are forgotten, the story of Purim will remain." These words, written by an unknown Biblical scholar of the Middle Ages, are as meaningful today as they were then. Purim is a timeless story, symbolic of the history of the Jewish people.

In the Book of Esther, the figure of Haman, the Persian King's minister, is typical of the countless number of persecutors who, having risen to a position of power, tried to exterminate the Jews. The Festival of Purim commemorates their miraculous survival and is a day of rejoicing and merrymaking.

The Haman Knocker has become as much a part of the celebrations as the masquerade parties and entertaining Purim plays. The traditional handmade wooden noisemaker is knocked back and forth, hitting the imaginary head of Haman and clapping with such force that the deafening noise is supposed to blot out any mention of his name.

MATERIALS:

Use white pine or basswood for the following: 1 pc. ¾″ x 5″ square for the platform; 1 pc. ¾″ x 2¼″ square for the knocker; 2 pcs. ¼″ x 1⅛″ x 8″, and 1 pc. ¼″ x 1⅛″ x 6¼″ lattice stock for the handle; 1 pc. ¼″ x 1⅛″ x 2⅝″ lattice stock for the arm; 1—¾″–18 wire nail; white glue.

Note: The original toy was made with a one-piece handle notched to fit the knocker arm. Making the handle with three pieces of lattice stock as indicated on the drawing simplifies the construction. Lattice stock is available at lumberyards. Dimensions may vary slightly in thickness and width. Cut mortises in knocker and platform to fit stock used.

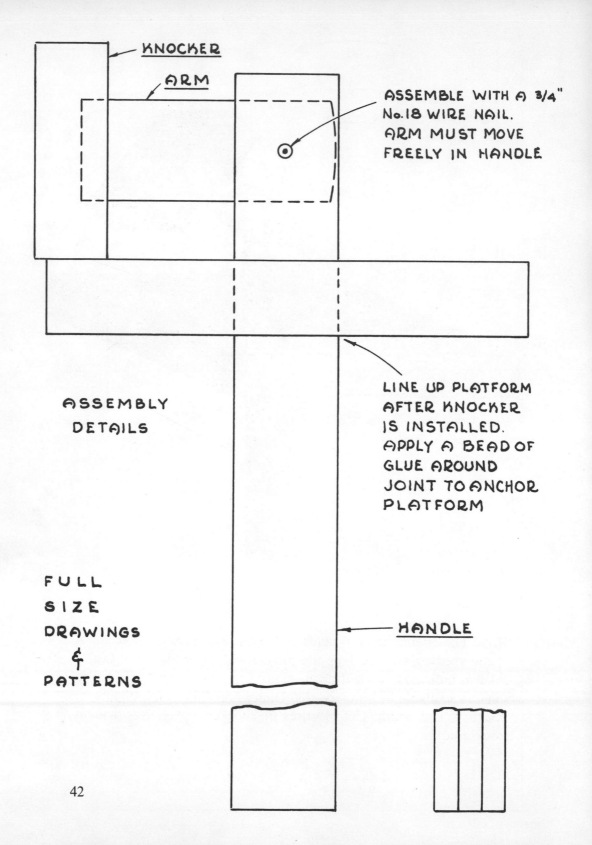

KNOCKER

ARM

ASSEMBLE WITH A 3/4"
No. 18 WIRE NAIL.
ARM MUST MOVE
FREELY IN HANDLE

ASSEMBLY
DETAILS

LINE UP PLATFORM
AFTER KNOCKER
IS INSTALLED.
APPLY A BEAD OF
GLUE AROUND
JOINT TO ANCHOR
PLATFORM

FULL
SIZE
DRAWINGS
&
PATTERNS

HANDLE

42

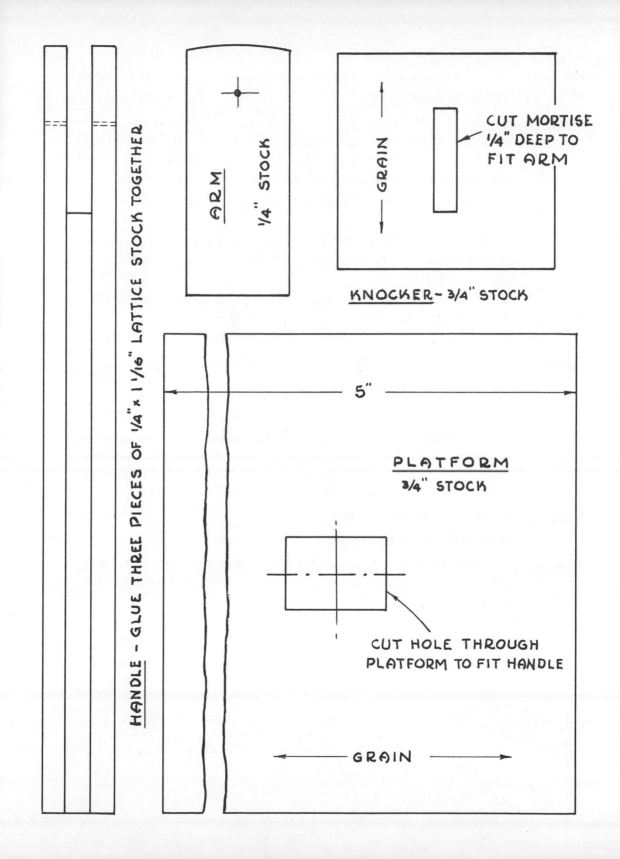

HANDLE – GLUE THREE PIECES OF 1/4" x 1 1/16" LATTICE STOCK TOGETHER

ARM
1/4" STOCK

KNOCKER – 3/4" STOCK

GRAIN

CUT MORTISE 1/4" DEEP TO FIT ARM

5"

PLATFORM
3/4" STOCK

CUT HOLE THROUGH PLATFORM TO FIT HANDLE

GRAIN

HOW TO MAKE IT:

1. Cut all parts to size.

2. Glue the three handle pieces together, keeping the ends flush at the bottom. Use white glue. Clamp or wrap with twine until glue dries. Remove excess glue with a damp cloth.

3. Chisel or carve the mortise in the knocker block to fit the knocker arm.

4. Drill the nail holes in the handle and knocker arm with a 1¼″–18 wire nail held in a hand drill. Cut off head of nail first; use pointed end as a drill.

5. Glue the arm in the knocker mortise, being sure it is perpendicular to the knocker surface. Allow glue to dry.

6. Cut the hole in the center of the platform to fit the handle. Drill a ¼″ hole through the wood first, then saw out the opening with a coping saw, or use a power jig saw. The platform should be a sliding fit on the handle.

7. Assemble the knocker in the handle notch. Drive the nail through the parts carefully. Knocker arm must swing freely in the handle.

8. Slide the platform on the handle, align it with the knocker as shown on the drawing, then apply a bead of white glue around the joint to secure the parts.

9. Paint or decorate to suit.

TO USE YOUR KNOCKER:

The handle may be held in a horizontal or vertical position. Swing the knocker from side to side with a wrist motion to make a clapping sound.

CORN COB DONKEY FROM
VENEZUELA–MEXICO

In the Spanish-speaking areas of South America, there is an unmistakable similarity in the traditional folk toys of children, but the stories of their origin differ from one country to the next.

The corn-husk donkey, loaded with stick crates, is a favorite of youngsters and a popular craft project on a rainy afternoon. Boys and girls, as well as men and women, take pride in their artistic creations: the twist of a long ear, the stiffness of the donkey's short-haired mane, even the shape and size of the cob—all combine to create a distinctly different animal with a definite character of its own.

In Venezuela, the corn-cob pack animal is said to have been made by the Indians of the area long before the Spaniards arrived—of course there were no horses in the Americas until the Spaniards introduced them—and it is held up as a reflection of the life of its creators, who used the sturdy little animal to carry their heavy loads up and down the mountainous countryside. Venezuelans maintain that this corn-cob animal is a uniquely *Venezuelan* toy.

A study of *Mexican* folk art, though, reveals another story of the toy's origin. In the days before the railway, long lines of mules would travel between the port of Acapulco and Mexico City. The arrival of the mule trains from the seaport to the main plaza of the capital city traditionally coincided with the outdoor festivities of Corpus Christi.

This festival has been a favorite since Colonial times. The boys adorn themselves in Indian pre-Columbian costumes; on their backs they carry small crates filled with colorful fruits and decorated with vivid sweet-scented flowers. Then they join the endless procession

45

that parades through the city, winding their way through the streets until they reach the main plaza of the town.

The traditional Corpus Christi mule is as much a part of the festive holiday today as it was. And hardly a Mexican child has not owned a little corn-husk mule laden with artificial fruits and flowers in stick crates, which are tiny replicas of the ones carried by the boys.

The quaint little corn-husk animal is a seasonal delight in Mexico; by replacing the husk with the cob, it is a traditional folk toy of Venezuela. But most of all, a pack animal made from an ear of corn is truly a Spanish-American creation.

MATERIALS:

1 or 2 dried corncobs for the body, neck, head; green cornhusks for the brooms and saddle blanket; corn silk or fine thread for broom ties; scrubbing brush bristles or sisal rope strands for the mane and tail; string or thread for the packsaddle straps; 4—¼″ x 3⅛″ wood dowels for the legs; 4—⅛″ x 3½″ wood dowels or split bamboo for

broom handles; 1—¼″ x 2¼″ wood dowel for the head-neck-body dowel pin; small pieces of corn husk or thin leather for the ears; 4 pcs. ¹⁄₁₆″ x ¼″ x 1⅞″ pine, balsa, basswood, or split bamboo for the packsaddle ends; 4 pcs. ¹⁄₁₆″ x ¼″ x 1¼″ of the same material for the packsaddle sides; white glue; black model paint.

HOW TO MAKE IT:

1. Cut the dried corn cobs into pieces for the body, neck, and head. Use the drawing for suggested sizes.

2. Drill the ¼″ holes for the dowel pin in the head and body about ½″ deep. Drill the neck hole through the center of the neck piece. Test-assemble the three pieces with the dowel pin for fit.

3. Drill the ¼″ leg holes in the body at an angle. Test-fit legs. Cut bevels on the bottoms of the legs so the animal will stand without wobbling.

4. Drill the ¼″ hole for the tail about ½″ deep.

5. Make a saw cut in the back of the head and neck pieces for the mane.

6. Glue the legs in the body.

7. Glue the head and neck together with the dowel pin, then glue the mane in place; use brush bristles, corn silk, or sisal rope strands for the mane.

8. Drill two ⅛″ holes for the ears. Glue the ears in position.

9. Glue the head and neck assembly in the body.

10. Make the tail using sisal rope strands. Glue in hole.

11. Make the packsaddle. Glue the end pieces together at 90°—see drawing detail. Allow glue to dry. Then add saddle sides, gluing them in position carefully.

12. Make the saddle blanket using several layers of corn husk. Glue on back of mule.

13. Glue packsaddle in position on the blanket. Make a cinch strap by folding a 12″ length of string or heavy thread in two, looping it around one side of the packsaddle, under the belly, then fasten it to the other side with a knot. Run another string from the rear of the packsaddle where the frame ends cross, around and under the tail,

then fasten it to the packsaddle frame at the same spot.

14. Make four brooms. Take a 5" to 6" length of corn husk and roll it around a ⅛" dowel until the roll is about ⅜" diameter. Apply a little glue to hold it in a roll. Next cut the roll into four 1¼" lengths and glue each piece on the end of a broom handle. Wrap the husks with thread over the broom handle area—see drawing.

15. Tie the brooms into two bundles of two brooms each, using thread wrappings at both ends—see drawing.

16. Glue the brooms in position at the neck and packsaddle.

17. Paint the bottoms of the legs black to resemble hoofs. Draw the eyes and mouth with paint or pencil.

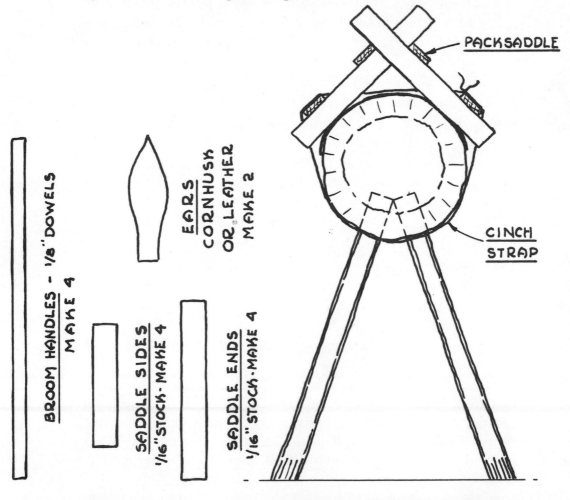

BROOM HANDLES - ⅛" DOWELS
MAKE 4

EARS
CORNHUSK
OR LEATHER
MAKE 2

SADDLE SIDES
'/16"STOCK - MAKE 4

SADDLE ENDS
'/16" STOCK - MAKE 4

PACKSADDLE

CINCH
STRAP

SECTION AT PACKSADDLE

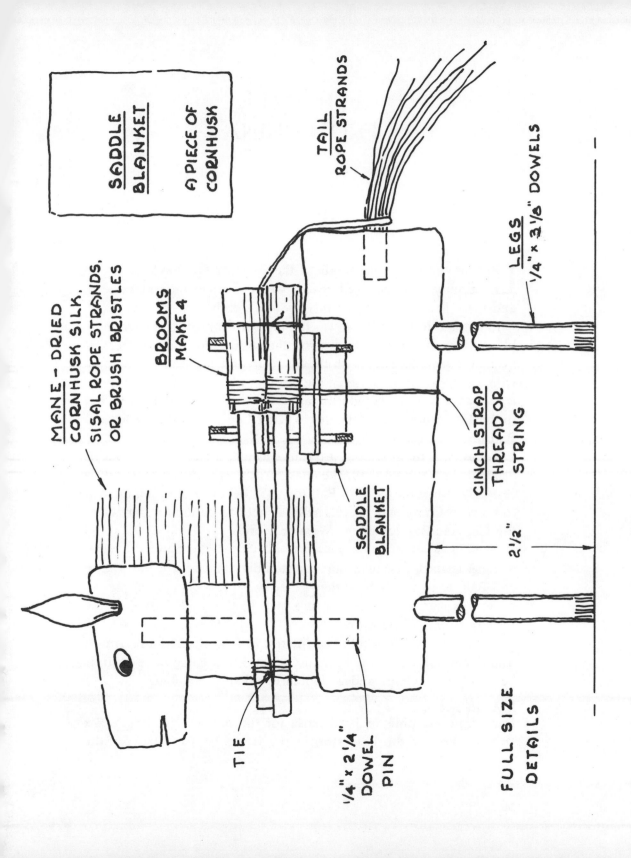

SADDLE
BLANKET
A PIECE OF CORNHUSK

TAIL
ROPE STRANDS

MANE — DRIED
CORNHUSK SILK,
SISAL ROPE STRANDS,
OR BRUSH BRISTLES

BROOMS
MAKE 4

SADDLE
BLANKET

CINCH STRAP
THREAD OR
STRING

LEGS
1/4" x 3 1/8" DOWELS

2 1/2"

TIE

1/4" x 2 1/4" DOWEL
PIN

FULL SIZE
DETAILS

FLIP BALL
FROM CHINA

Like many folk toys, the origin of the Cup and Ball has been lost in antiquity. It is believed that it was known in ancient Greece, and there is evidence it was in Italy at an early date.

In the late 16th century it was the rage of France: King Henry III played Cup and Ball as he walked the streets and the members of his Court were obsessed with the toy. Cup and Ball was fashionable with the upper class, and even the most humble peasant of the countryside took to it. Its popularity lasted for over a hundred years, and in the 18th century the daughter of King Louis XIV had a Cup and Ball toy.

Today, it is thought of as a traditional folk toy of Mexico, but its original home points to the East. Although documentation is certainly scarce on the Flip-Ball toy, it is believed to be an ancient folk toy of China and, traditionally, is held to be the forerunner of the Cup-and-Ball toy of the Western world.

In 1778, when Captain James Cook visited the Sandwich (Hawaiian) Islands, he noted that the islanders played a form of Cup and Ball. Ring and Ball, as they called the toy, was made of plaited cane; this appears to have been a step in the modification of the Eastern to the Western toy.

Today, as a result of renewed interest in folk arts and a revival in traditional folk crafts, the ancient Cup-and-Ball game once again is being made in China and is popularly called "Flip Ball."

MATERIALS:
Use basswood, pine, or hard balsa for the following: 1 pc. $3/16''$ x $13/16''$ x $14\frac{1}{2}''$ for the base strip; 1 pc. $\frac{1}{8}''$ x $13/16''$ x $10\frac{7}{8}''$ for the

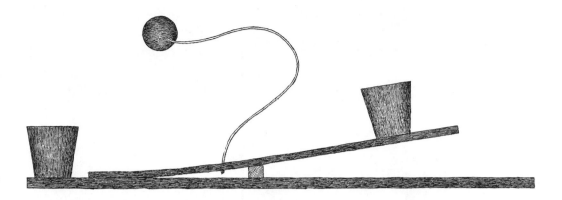

spring strip; 1 pc. $^{5/16}''$ x $^{3}\!/_{8}''$ x $^{13/16}''$ for the spacing block; 2 pcs. 1⅛″ square x 1¼″ for the tubs; 1 pc. string about 8″ long; 1—¾″ diameter wood bead; 2—½″-20 wire brads or nails; white glue.

HOW TO MAKE IT:

1. Cut base and spring strips to size. Note the spring strip is thinner than the base strip. (A basswood yardstick will supply material for these pieces.) Round one end of each piece as shown on the top view of the drawing; leave the other ends square. Sand both pieces smooth.

2. Drill a $^{1/16}''$ dia. hole for the string in the center of the spring strip at the position indicated on the drawing.

3. Make the spacing block; glue it to the base strip at the position shown on the side view of the drawing.

4. Mark the position of the square end of the spring strip on the base strip. Apply white glue over the area indicated, then clamp the strips together at the joint until the glue dries overnight. Sides of strips should be flush.

5. Drive the two ½″ brads through both pieces at the points shown to reinforce the glue joint. Clip off the excess length on the underside of the strips, then flatten the ends with a hammer, supporting the top side with a piece of metal or hardwood to keep the brads from loosening.

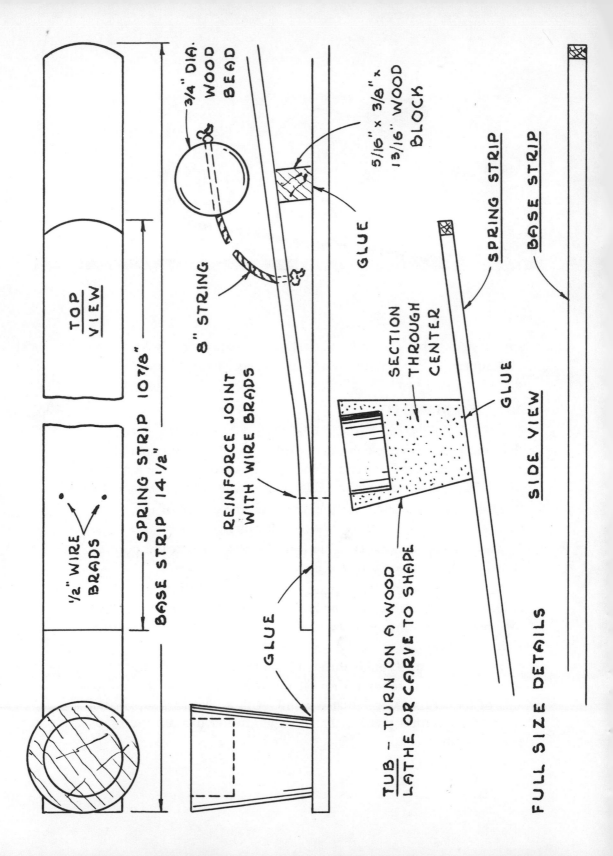

TOP VIEW

SPRING STRIP 10 7/8"

BASE STRIP 14 1/2"

1/2" WIRE BRADS

3/4" DIA. WOOD BEAD

8" STRING

5/16" x 3/8" x 13/16" WOOD BLOCK

GLUE

GLUE

REINFORCE JOINT WITH WIRE BRADS

GLUE

SECTION THROUGH CENTER

SPRING STRIP

BASE STRIP

GLUE

TUB – TURN ON A WOOD LATHE OR CARVE TO SHAPE

SIDE VIEW

FULL SIZE DETAILS

6. Make the two tubs. They can be made by hand or preferably turned on a wood lathe equipped with a screw center or faceplate. The original toy tubs were turned on a wood lathe. If made by hand, bore $13/16''$ dia. holes in the ends of the blocks first, then carve or sand the blocks to a tub shape. Square tubs can be substituted if desired. If turned on a wood lathe, drill pilot holes for the screw center in one end of the blocks, then use turning tools to cut the ball recess in the top ends and the taper on the sides. Sand smooth before removing from machine.

7. Apply white glue to the bottoms of the tubs. Clamp in position on the spring and base strips as shown on the side view of the drawing until glue dries.

8. Thread the string through the wood bead and spring strip. Knot both ends.

9. The original toy was left unpainted. You can paint yours if you prefer.

TO USE YOUR FLIP BALL:

Hold the toy in either hand. Place the bead in the spring strip tub. Place your thumb on the rounded end of the spring strip, squeeze strips together, then slide your thumb quickly toward your hand. How many times will you have to try before you catch the bead in the forward tub? It takes skill and patience!

THE HANGMAN'S NOOSE
FROM FRANCE

The Hangman's Noose, known in France as *Le Pendu,* is one of the most intriguing and fascinating folk toys. And it is one of those toys with a political background.

Inspired by the French Revolution and aimed at the terrorists, it was a satirical take-off mocking the mass beheadings on the guillotine. The simple, original version became popular so rapidly that before long it was developed into a more sophisticated toy.

Within the first few years of its creation it crossed the Atlantic, becoming one of the most popular toys of the Appalachian Mountain children. Here its basic form was kept, but the Americans rechristened it with the whimsical name "Flipperdinger."

Le Pendu or the Flipperdinger is one of those folk toys that can easily compete with the most modern manufactured toys of our industrial age. It can be made within a short time and is well worth the effort, for it is lots of fun and has the curious power of being able to absorb your attention completely.

MATERIALS:

1 pc. ¾″ x 5¼″ square pine or basswood for the platform; 1 pc. ¼″ x 7″ wood dowel for the post; 1 pc. ¼″ x 3½″ wood dowel for the arm; 1 pc. string or carpet thread for the noose; 1 pc. ¾″ dia. soft balsa for the ball; 1—3″ length #18 copper wire or straightened paper clip for the ball hook; 1 pc. ½″ x 7″ plastic tubing for the mouthpiece; 1 pc. ¼″ x 1¾″ plastic tubing for the blow tube; Duco-type cement or white glue.

HOW TO MAKE IT:

1. Cut the 45° bevels on the post and arm dowels. Glue together with white glue or Duco-type cement. Set aside on waxed paper to dry. Check to see that pieces join at 90°. Note: A piece of coat hanger wire may be substituted for the post and arm. In this case, bend the wire in an L-shape following the sizes shown on the drawing and drill the post hole in the platform to fit the wire.

2. Draw a 5″ diameter circle on the platform block, then draw centerlines for the three holes and drill as indicated on the drawing. Saw out disc with a coping saw or use a power jig saw.

3. Remove saw marks with fine sandpaper. Round edges slightly.

4. If toy is to be painted, apply paint to wood parts before final assembly.

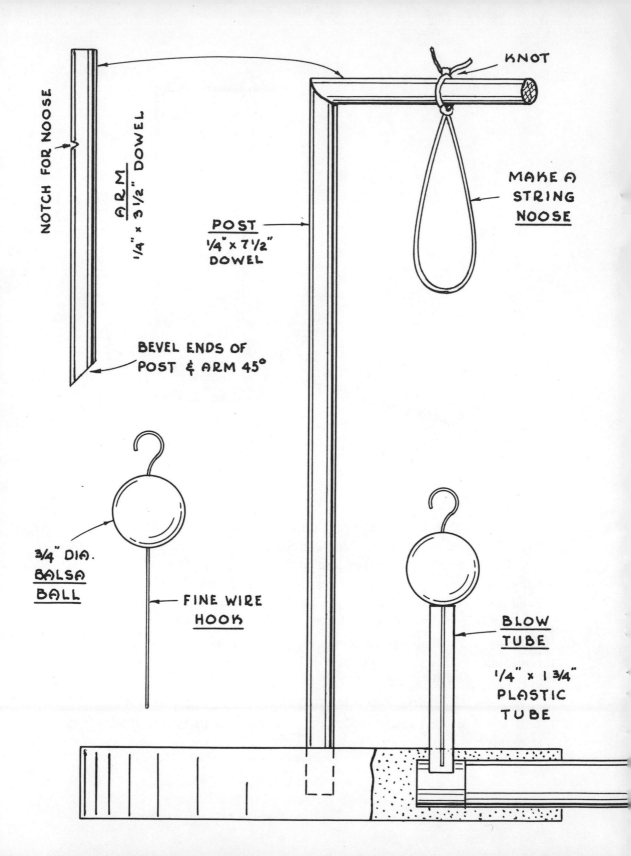

NOTCH FOR NOOSE

ARM
1/4" × 3 1/2" DOWEL

POST
1/4" × 7 1/2"
DOWEL

BEVEL ENDS OF
POST & ARM 45°

3/4" DIA.
BALSA
BALL

FINE WIRE
HOOK

KNOT

MAKE A
STRING
NOOSE

BLOW
TUBE

1/4" × 1 3/4"
PLASTIC
TUBE

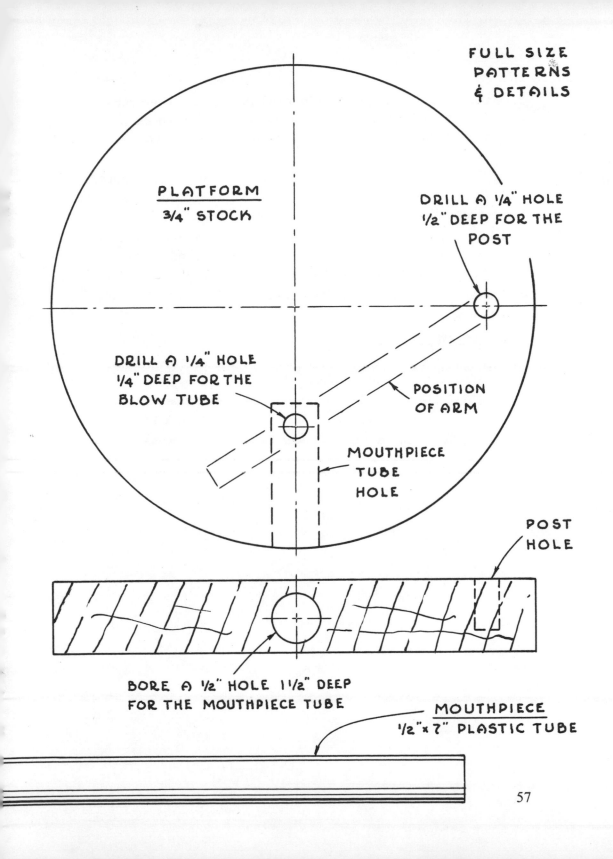

PLATFORM
3/4" STOCK

DRILL A 1/4" HOLE
1/2" DEEP FOR THE
POST

DRILL A 1/4" HOLE
1/4" DEEP FOR THE
BLOW TUBE

POSITION
OF ARM

MOUTHPIECE
TUBE
HOLE

POST
HOLE

BORE A 1/2" HOLE 11/2" DEEP
FOR THE MOUTHPIECE TUBE

MOUTHPIECE
1/2" x 7" PLASTIC TUBE

57

5. Make the ball and wire hook next. Carve and sand the ball to shape. Bend the hook on one end of the wire, then push the other end through the center of the ball, locating it as shown on the drawing.

6. Begin assembly by pressing the mouthpiece tube in the platform disc about 1", the blow tube about ¼". Apply a bead of Duco cement around the blow tube to reinforce the joint.

7. Glue the post and arm assembly in the platform hole, lining up the arm so the noose notch is directly above the blow tube. The post should be perpendicular to the platform disc surface.

8. Make a string or thread noose and tie it to the arm at the noose notch.

HOW TO OPERATE LE PENDU:

Place the ball and wire hook in the plastic blow tube. Now, blowing in short puffs into the mouthpiece, blow the ball upward until the hook hangs on the noose. It may take several tries until you can control your breath enough to hook it the first time. For more fun, see if you can blow the ball off the noose and return it to the blow tube.

DARUMA DOLLS
FROM JAPAN

A book on toys would not be complete without at least a glimpse into toyland, and Japan, home of the largest toy industry in the world, is virtually just that.

One of the country's best known folk toys is the Daruma. The toy is named after Bodhidharma (Dharma), a 6th century Indian Buddhist who is credited as the founder of Zen Buddhism.

The teachings of Zen developed from Buddhism, but Zen is a way of life rather than an organized religion. Zen stresses the importance of meditation, and its practice requires rigid discipline; its goal is to acquire an inner serenity and a balanced and orderly daily existence.

The principles of Zen are carried out in the design of Japanese gardens where simplicity is emphasized; seen in Japanese flower arranging—*Ikebana*; form a part of the traditional Japanese tea ceremony; and are even practiced in such sports as archery, judo and swordsmanship.

Dharma, therefore, has earned a most prominent place in Japan's cultural heritage, and the Daruma toy typifies his elevated position, for it is constructed so that no matter how it is pushed, it rolls about until it lands in an upright position.

According to legend, Dharma sat immobile and meditated for nine years. This resulted in a paralysis so severe that he lost the use of his arms and legs. There are stories that say he rolled all the way from India to Japan to spread his teachings.

There are many different kinds of darumas: "Bean dolls" are constructed in the same way as more traditional darumas. The name

"bean" merely refers to the toy's small size. These self-righting dolls, decorated in dark blue and bright red, are made in pairs to keep each other company; they are regarded as the symbol of two happy people.

In northern Japan, a very elaborate daruma is made with glass eyes and real hair.

Some darumas are made in the form of masks, representing long-nosed goblins and foxes. These are sold at fairs to farmers who use them as scarecrows to protect their melon crops.

The Toyooka darumas look like cats and symbolize good fortune. Their name comes from the town where a Buddhist priest is said to have carved a wooden daruma to bring good luck to a farmer.

Yearly, brightly colored daruma dolls are sold at the daruma market in Tokyo, and many darumas are made for the celebration of the Japanese New Year. Some are thought to be charms against illness and for the healthy growth of children; others are symbolic of recovery from ill fortune. In some parts of Japan "woman" darumas are thrown into the homes of friends to bring happy New Year wishes.

One of the most charming traditions associated with this folk toy is the "wishing" daruma, made without eyes. When a child makes a wish, he paints in one eye, and the daruma is given his second eye only after the wish has come true.

There are innumerable ways of making darumas. The simplest to make is the "triangular" daruma, which is made by setting a paper cone into a clay base. Once the clay has set, the details of the face are carefully painted on the cone. These "triangular" darumas are traditionally colored in either red or blue.

Note: The original daruma doll was made of baked clay. To simplify construction, this version of the toy is made with one-half a rubber ball filled with plaster of Paris or modeling clay, which will give the base weight and righting qualities whenever the toy is tipped. The dolls can be made any size depending on the diameter of the ball. Cone-shaped and tapered-side paper drinking cups may be substituted for bodies also.

MATERIALS:

1—2" diameter rubber ball, or sponge rubber ball, for the bases; plaster of Paris or modeling clay; 2 pcs. 4" x 6" colored paper or file cards for the cones; ½" masking tape or colored plastic tape; white glue or Duco-type cement; assorted model paints or colored felt pens.

HOW TO MAKE THEM:

1. Carefully cut the ball in two with a sharp modeler's knife or single-edge razor blade using the mold seam as a guide. Use one half for one doll base. If a sponge rubber ball is used, omit the next step.

2. Fill the ball halves with plaster of Paris or modeling clay level with the top. If plaster is used, allow it to dry at least overnight before adding the paper cones.

3. Duplicating the cone pattern, use a compass and ruler to draw the cone outlines on the paper or card stock. Cut blanks with scissors.

4. Roll the blanks to form cones, then glue edges together along the glue flap.

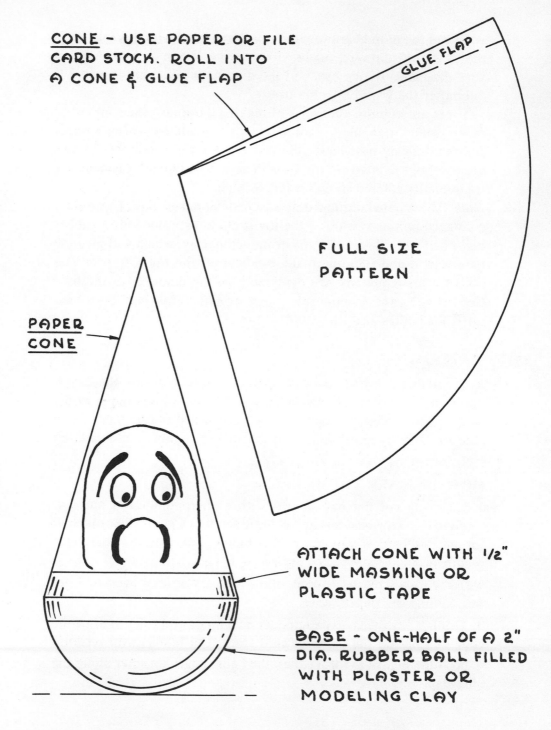

CONE – USE PAPER OR FILE CARD STOCK. ROLL INTO A CONE & GLUE FLAP

GLUE FLAP

FULL SIZE PATTERN

PAPER CONE

ATTACH CONE WITH 1/2" WIDE MASKING OR PLASTIC TAPE

BASE – ONE-HALF OF A 2" DIA. RUBBER BALL FILLED WITH PLASTER OR MODELING CLAY

5. Fasten the cones to the bases with masking tape or colored plastic tape.

6. Paint face details, or use colored felt pens to decorate.

An alternate way to decorate the cones would be to do the art work before the paper is formed into a cone.

TO OPERATE YOUR DARUMAS:

Place them on a flat surface, then touch them at the top of the cones and watch them roll and roll and roll. Move the top of the cones in a slight circle and see what happens. Or set darumas side by side and tip their tops together. Lay them on their sides and see what happens. Set them on a slight slanting surface and tip them sideways. Will they roll over or work their way down the ramp?

PRISONER'S LOCK
FROM FINLAND

If an intriguing object that can be played with for hours on end fits the definition of a toy, then the Prisoner's Lock has a definite place in this book. It is exhibited in the National Museum of Finland as a traditional folk toy. But the Finns are the first to admit its foreign origin; their claim to the lock is based only on its continued popularity in Finland over the last 150 years. Both children and adults find the lock a perfect pastime during the long, cold winter nights in the Land of the Midnight Sun. It is a most ingenious device and can be solved only with a great deal of patience.

The story of its origin is a most romantic one. It is said that the Prussian Baron, Frederick Von der Trenck, was in love with the sister of King Frederick the Great. The Prussian King, suspecting the Baron of having only dishonorable intentions, imprisoned him for ten years. It was here that the unfortunate Baron is said to have invented the Prisoner's Lock, which later became known as Trenck's Lock.

Further research on the part of the Finns has led them to believe that during the first decade of the 19th century, a secret agent of the English army, Major Malcolm Sinclair, invented this fascinating puzzle; thus evolved its modern Finnish name, Sinclair's Lock.

In England, however, Chinese Rings, as the lock is called, was known at least as early as the 18th century. Does this name give a clue to its country of origin? Perhaps, but this deduction would be far more convincing if it had not been known in Italy in the 16th century. Italians credit its invention to their outstanding mathematician

Geronimo Cardan, and call the lock "Cardan's Rings." In France *Le Baguenaudier*—Ring Puzzle—was originally used as an effective device to deter burglars; and in Norway it has been used for centuries as a lock on boxes.

MATERIALS:

1 pc. ¼″ x 1½″ x 6½″ pine or basswood for the base (lock); 7—1″ diameter curtain or key rings; 7—3″ lengths of #14 copper or .880″ iron wire for the pins; 1—14¼″ length of lightweight coat hanger wire for the bar; 1—½″ wood bead.

HOW TO MAKE IT:

1. Make the base. Lay out centers and drill the seven ⅛″ holes as shown on the drawing. Number the holes from 1 to 7.

2. Make seven ring and pin assemblies. Bend a ¼″ loop at one end of each wire with a pair of round nose pliers, insert a ring in the loop, then squeeze loop shut.

3. Insert one ring and pin assembly through hole 7. Bend a second loop at the end of the wire under the base.

4. Hold ring 7 so it encircles hole 6, then insert another ring and pin unit through hole 6 and bend the second loop as before.

5. Hold ring 6 so it encircles hole 5, then install a ring and pin through hole 5 in the same manner.

6. Continue installing the rest of the ring and pin units, using the same procedure. When finished, ring 1 should overlap ring 2, ring 2 should overlap ring 3, etcetera.

7. Make the bar. Bend the clotheshanger wire and install the wood bead as shown on the drawing.

HOW TO HOLD THE LOCK AND BAR:

Hold the base (lock) and bar in front of you with both hands so the bead on the bar and hole 7 in the base are on the right. Now hold the base in your left hand, supporting it by the third and fourth fingers and with pins 1 and 2 between these fingers. Use your thumb and first finger to hold the base firm on top and to manipulate the rings. Use your right hand to move the bar, pushing it toward hole 1 to go forward, toward hole 7 to pull back.

HOW TO SOLVE THE PUZZLE:

OBJECT: To close and open the lock. The lock is closed when all rings are looped over the bar as shown in the artist's sketch. It is open when the bar is removed from all the rings.

RULES:

1. Rings must be added to the bar in numerical sequence 1 to 7, removed in reverse sequence 7 to 1.

2. Rings may be picked up (added) or dropped (removed) one or two at a time.

TO PICK UP A RING, slide it UP diagonally between the wires of the bar (bar slot), pull the bar back until the ring drops DOWN over the END of the bar, then push the bar forward THROUGH the ring. Rings 1 and 2 are picked up the same way.

TO DROP A RING, pull the bar back until it touches a pin, lift the ring UP, push the bar forward UNDER the ring, then slide the ring DOWN diagonally between the wires (bar slot). Rings 1 and 2 are dropped the same way.

3. In order to pick up or drop a ring, the ring PRECEDING it must be on the bar, for example: To pick up or drop ring 3, ring 2 must be on the bar (ring 1 must be off). To pick up or drop ring 7, ring 6 must be on the bar (rings 1,2,3,4 and 5 must be off). For a few moves, more than one ring may be on the bar at the same time.

4. There are no shortcuts to closing or opening the lock. The solutions give the correct sequences which must be followed. It takes 66

moves to close the lock and 64 moves to open it.

TO CLOSE THE LOCK—SOLUTION:

Pick up ring 1:
Slide ring 1 diagonally up through the bar slot with the thumb and first finger of the left hand and hold it horizontally on top of the wires. Pull the bar back until it touches the pin, then slide it forward so it goes through the ring. Ring 1 is now on the bar.

Next, add ring 2:
Slide ring 2 up through the bar slot and hold it on top of the wires. Pull the bar back to pin 1, drop ring 2 over the end of the bar, then slide the bar forward again through both rings. Now you have two rings on the bar.

Now add ring 3, using this code:
Drop 1, pick up 3, pick up 1.

To add ring 4:
Drop 1 and 2, pick up 4, pick up 1 and 2.

And for ring 5:
Drop 1, drop 3, pick up 1, drop 1 and 2, pick up 5, pick up 1 and 2, drop 1, pick up 3, pick up 1. You should now have five rings on the bar.

To pick up ring 6:
Drop 1 and 2, drop 4, pick up 1 and 2, drop 1, drop 3, pick up 1, drop 1 and 2, pick up 6, pick up 1 and 2, drop 1, pick up 3, pick up 1, drop 1 and 2, pick up 4, pick up 1 and 2. Check. Six rings should be on the bar.

Now, to add ring 7:
Drop 1, drop 3, pick up 1, drop 1 and 2, drop 5, pick up 1 and 2, drop 1, pick up 3, pick up 1, drop 1 and 2, drop 4, pick up 1 and 2, drop 1, drop 3, pick up 1, drop 1 and 2, pick up 7, pick up 1 and 2, drop 1, pick up 3, pick up 1, drop 1 and 2, pick up 4, pick up 1 and 2, drop 1, drop 3, pick up 1, drop 1 and 2, pick up 5, pick up 1 and 2, drop 1, pick up 3, pick up 1. The lock is closed if you have seven rings on the bar.

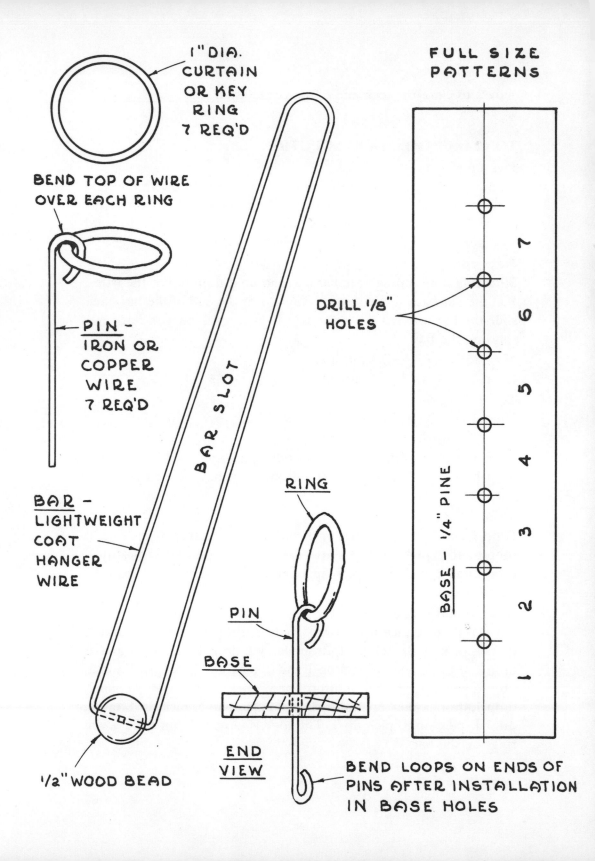

1" DIA. CURTAIN OR KEY RING 7 REQ'D

FULL SIZE PATTERNS

BEND TOP OF WIRE OVER EACH RING

PIN — IRON OR COPPER WIRE 7 REQ'D

BAR SLOT

BAR — LIGHTWEIGHT COAT HANGER WIRE

DRILL 1/8" HOLES

7 6 5 4 3 2 1

BASE — 1/4" PINE

RING

PIN

BASE

1/2" WOOD BEAD

END VIEW

BEND LOOPS ON ENDS OF PINS AFTER INSTALLATION IN BASE HOLES

TO OPEN THE LOCK—SOLUTION:

Start with seven rings on the bar, then:

Drop 1, drop 3, pick up 1, drop 1 and 2, drop 5, pick up 1 and 2, drop 1, pick up 3, pick up 1, drop 1 and 2, drop 4, pick up 1 and 2, drop 1, drop 3, pick up 1, drop 1 and 2, drop 7. Only ring 6 is now on the bar. Pick up 1 and 2, drop 1, pick up 3, pick up 1, drop 1 and 2, pick up 4, pick up 1 and 2, drop 1, drop 3, pick up 1, drop 1 and 2, pick up 5, pick up 1 and 2, drop 1, pick up 3, pick up 1, drop 1 and 2, drop 4, pick up 1 and 2, drop 1, drop 3, pick up 1, drop 1 and 2, drop 6. Only ring 5 is now on the bar. Pick up 1 and 2, drop 1, pick up 3, pick up 1, drop 1 and 2, pick up 4, pick up 1 and 2, drop 1, drop 3, pick up 1, drop 1 and 2, drop 5. Only ring 4 is now on the bar. Pick up 1 and 2, drop 1, pick up 3, pick up 1, drop 1 and 2, drop 4. Only ring 3 is now on the bar. Pick up 1 and 2, drop 1, drop 3. Only ring 2 is left on the bar. Pick up 1, drop 1 and 2. Lock is open! Now try closing and opening the lock without looking at the solution.

A SHADOW PUPPET FROM INDONESIA (JAVA)

The Shadow Play, it is believed, was born in India; some scholars, however, maintain it originated in China or Japan. But regardless of its origin, the art of Shadowgraphy matured and reached the height of perfection in Java. And it is the *Wayang Kulit,* the Javanese shadow figures cut from uncured leather of water-buffalo skin, that reveal the history of nine centuries of Javanese culture.

The Shadow Play was well known in Java by the 11th century, and then, as now, a performance of the legendary story of the *Ramayana* was a favorite form of entertainment.

The Hindu epic, the *Ramayana,* originated in India, but became so much a part of Javanese culture that today it is referred to as the National Reader of the people. Yet, it seems incongruous that the island of Java, which is predominantly Moslem, would choose a Hindu epic as the traditional story of their theatre.

But when the *Ramayana* was first introduced into Java, the people of the island were predominantly followers of Hinduism. And the story appealed to them because they identified its heroes with their own mythical ancestors. They admired the good King Rama, the protector of the weak and the poor; and they respected the purity of Queen Sita, who still remains the example of the perfect woman to Indonesian girls.

By the end of the 15th century, when the spread of Mohammedanism had peacefully engulfed the island of Java, the Shadow Play was too much a part of the people to be erased. It was prohibited by Islam as being a creation of the pre-Moslem period; furthermore, the puppets were condemned as being sacrilegious, in contradiction

to the Koran—the Holy Book of Islam—which forbade the worship of idols or the making of portraits of living creatures. But a tradition of centuries could not suddenly cease to exist, and so, the artists compromised. The puppets were stylized and various heroes of Moslem literature were introduced.

On the nearby island of Bali, however, where Mohammedanism was never able to gain a foothold, the ancient Hindu form of the Wayang figures has been preserved.

To the Javanese, the Shadow Play is a mirror of life: man is but a moving shadow, a puppet in the hands of God. The Dalang, the narrator and director of the play, represents the creator of man, for it is he who puts the puppets into motion. He is the soul of each and every shadow on the white screen, which is called the Kelir. He, alone, is the actor, orator and singer; he is the stage manager and orchestra leader; the composer and dance master.

Today, the Dalang tells his enchanting story in Bahasa Indonesia, the national language of the country. His figures often have new faces, the popular personalities of the day; but his theme has not changed, the forces of good and evil are still the tone of his message as he portrays the struggle of his people to remain united and keep their spirit of independence.

Whether the performance is the traditional play of yesterday, or a modernized version depicting life today, when the Dalang lights the flame of his oil lamp, there is silence. At 9 P.M. he brings out his first figure; the flickering flame casts its light on the translucent leather character. He has captured his audience. They never cease to be fascinated by the graceful movements of the shadowy shapes behind the fine white screen, for it is as if the Dalang has breathed life into the puppets he so skillfully controls.

MATERIALS:

1 pc. 5″ x 9″ goatskin rawhide about .020″ thick for the body and arms (leathercraft store)—or substitute tag stock or a high-quality drawing paper such as 3-ply Strathmore Bristol board; 1—24″ and 1—6½″ lengths of # 16 or 18 wire for the handles; masking or plastic tape; coat or button thread; sponge and water; waterproof tracing paper; hardwood block about 1″ x 8″ x 10″ for a cutting board; acrylic spray paint, clear, and assorted acrylic paints.

HOW TO MAKE IT:

Note: If Bristol board or tag stock is used, follow the same general procedure for cutting, but do not dampen the material.

72

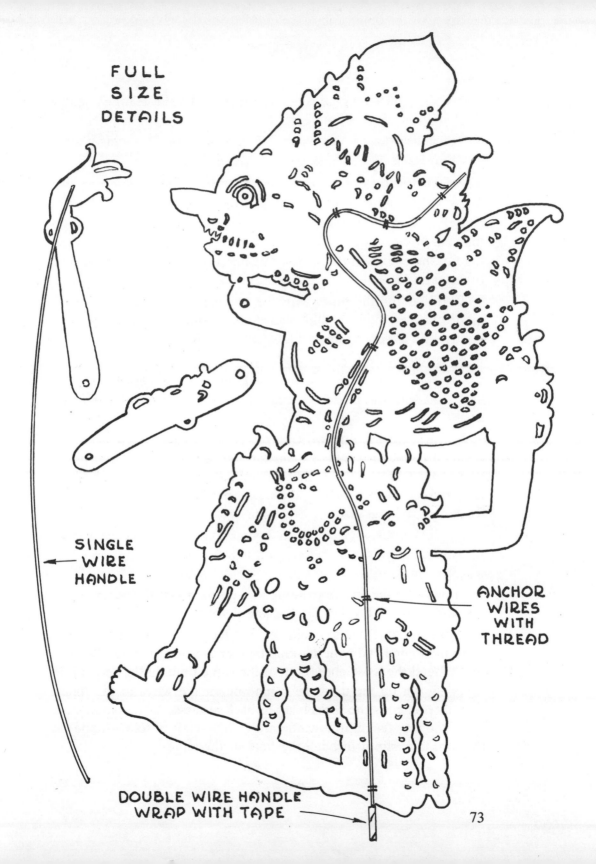

FULL
SIZE
DETAILS

SINGLE
WIRE
HANDLE

ANCHOR
WIRES
WITH
THREAD

DOUBLE WIRE HANDLE
WRAP WITH TAPE

73

1. Prepare goatskin by soaking it in water for 1 hour. Hang up to dry for 1 hour so air hits both sides freely.

2. Trace the drawing on a piece of 7″ x 9″ waterproof tracing paper.

3. Thumbtack the rawhide at the corners to the cutting board.

4. Fasten the tracing paper in position over the rawhide at two corners so it can be lifted to dampen the rawhide occasionally.

5. Before cutting or punching holes in the rawhide, keep in mind that the holes in the body are not for decoration, but to allow the light to show through the parts to highlight details—for example—the bracelet and mouth.

6. Begin cutting the holes with the modeler's knife, or use home-made punches, made by filing nails to the contours needed. Hit them lightly with a 4-oz. hammer. Cut right through the tracing paper.

7. Keep the rawhide damp while it is being worked—NOT wet.

8. After all holes are cut or punched, cut the outlines of the body and arms with the modeler's knife—NOT scissors. Allow leather to dry.

9. For arm hinges, cut two tiny pieces of rawhide about $\frac{1}{16}$″x$\frac{3}{16}$″, dampen them, then thread them through the arm holes and pinch both sides with a pair of pliers to spread and flatten them. Allow leather to dry before moving arms. (For cardboard bodies, use string for hinges, tying a knot on each side of the joint.)

10. Lightly coat both sides of the body and arms with a clear acrylic spray, then allow to dry before painting. Hang the puppet on a fine wire for spraying.

11. Following the artist's painting as a guide, paint the puppet. Use fine sable artist's brushes for the fine details.

12. To make the handles, fold the 24″ length of wire in two, then wrap the folded end with masking tape or plastic tape for a distance of 4″. Bend the loose ends, both at the same time, in the serpentine shape shown on the drawings, then anchor the wires to the figure with thread, tying the wires back-to-back at the six points indicated. Bend the 6½″ length in a gentle arc with a small offset (S-shape) at the top, then slip it through the hole in the hand.

THUMB PIANO FROM
AFRICA (UGANDA)

The thumb piano, a uniquely African instrument, ranks with the xylophone as the most popular instrument on the African continent. Its actual place of origin is uncertain, although strong evidence indicates that it may have been first developed in the Congo region some 500 years ago. Also known as a finger xylophone, it's mainly played outside of Africa in areas such as the West Indies, where great numbers of Africans were shipped by slave traders from the 16th to the 19th century.

The thumb piano differs in size and shape from one country in Africa to the next, and although the basic principle of the over one hundred varieties is the same, the name varies according to locale. The one in the illustration from Uganda is known as a *Sansa* or *Zanza;* in central Africa it is called a *Mbira;* whereas in Tanzania it is called a *Lukembe* and in Nigeria an *Agidibo.* But regardless of its appearance and name, throughout Africa the tonal quality of the thumb piano is similar.

For many years Western musicologists regarded the thumb piano as a rhythm instrument, used in much the same way as we might clap our hands or tap our feet in time to a well known, catchy folk tune. Recent studies, however, have shown that this instrument has a very definite tonal scale based on five equal intervals. The length and position of each of the 8 to 36 thin metal strips, or keys, determine the tone of the note. The middle keys have the lowest tone, whereas, the outside keys become progressively higher in pitch.

The popularity and use of the thumb piano among African school children may be compared to our guitar; in Africa, however, children are taught not only how to play their instruments but how to make their own.

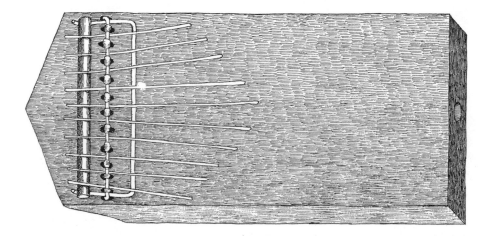

MATERIALS:

Use medium or hard balsa for these parts: 1 pc. ¼″ x 3¾″ x 9½″ for the top; 1 pc. ¼″ x 3¾″ x 7½″ for the bottom; 2 pcs. ¼″ x 1″ x 8¾″ for the sides; 2 pcs. ¼″ x 1″ x 3¼″ for the ends; 1 pc. ³⁄₁₆″ x 3″ wood dowel for the wood bridge; 1 pc. ³⁄₃₂″ x 6¼″ iron wire for the metal bridge; 1 pc. ¹⁄₁₆″ x 4″ iron wire for the anchor wire; 1—24″ length ⅛″ wide rattan—or use a thin rawhide shoelace—for the anchor wire tie-down; 1—36″ length .040″ x ¹⁄₁₆″ flat spring steel wire (locksmith, clock repair, or hardware store) for the keys. Cut 2 pcs. of each length: 4″, 3¾″, 3½″, 3¼″, and 3″; 16—¾″–18 wire brads; white glue.

HOW TO MAKE IT:

Note: The original thumb piano was made from a solid block of hard balsa, carved to shape on the outside and hollowed out on the inside to form a resonance chamber which was finally sealed with a thin piece of wood along one side. Since a block of balsa large enough to make this instrument may be unobtainable locally, a

76

built-up box design has been substituted for simplicity of construction. Also, the rattan lacing holes in the top were first drilled crudely, then burned clean with a red hot wire; this detail has been omitted. A diagonal slash-pattern was likewise burned along the sides of the top and bottom surfaces for decoration but has been omitted on the drawings.

1. Cut the wood pieces to size for the body of the instrument. Leave ends square on all parts until the body is assembled.

2. Locate and drill the ½″ holes in the bottom and one end as shown on the drawings.

3. Locate the end positions on the sides with both sides held together. Square guide lines across the sides on the inside surfaces. Note that sides overlap ends.

4. Lightly drive two ¾″–18 wire brads into the sides at each joint and into the end pieces just enough to anchor them, then apply glue at the joints and finish making the frame. Glue the frame to the bottom in the same manner, then add the top panel. Place a piece of scrap wood on top of the assembly and weight it down until the glue dries overnight.

5. Remove excess glue, then sand the box smooth.

6. Draw a light centerline on the top panel from end to end. Lay out the diamond point and the curves on the sides, then cut these contours, sanding them to a finish.

7. Lay out centerlines for the thirteen ⅛″ rattan lace holes in the top panel. These holes are spaced on ¼″ centers, starting at the centerline. Drill the holes, then countersink each carefully both top and bottom with a ³⁄₁₆″ drill twisted by hand. Sand surfaces smooth.

8. Make the metal bridge. Flatten the center portion of the wire as indicated on the bridge pattern drawing until it is ¹⁄₃₂″ thick. Use a ball-peen hammer, supporting the work by a piece of flat, heavy metal for an anvil. Bend the ends up 90°, also as shown, then form the bridge into a wide U-shape, using the top view drawing as a guide for the correct contour.

9. Soak the rattan in water until it is pliable, then, starting from the

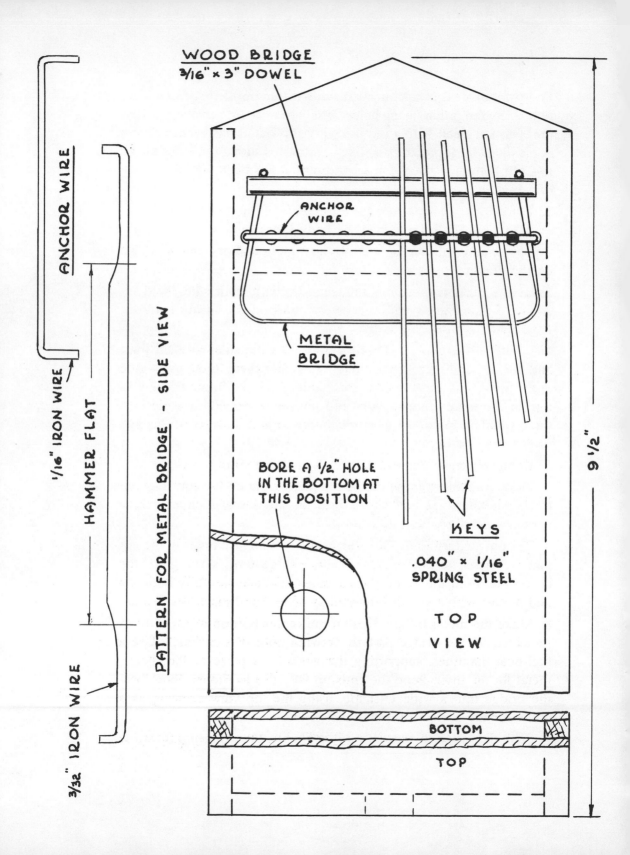

ANCHOR WIRE

1/16" IRON WIRE

HAMMER FLAT

PATTERN FOR METAL BRIDGE - SIDE VIEW

3/32" IRON WIRE

WOOD BRIDGE
3/16" × 3" DOWEL

ANCHOR WIRE

METAL BRIDGE

BORE A 1/2" HOLE
IN THE BOTTOM AT
THIS POSITION

KEYS

.040" × 1/16"
SPRING STEEL

TOP
VIEW

9 1/2"

BOTTOM

TOP

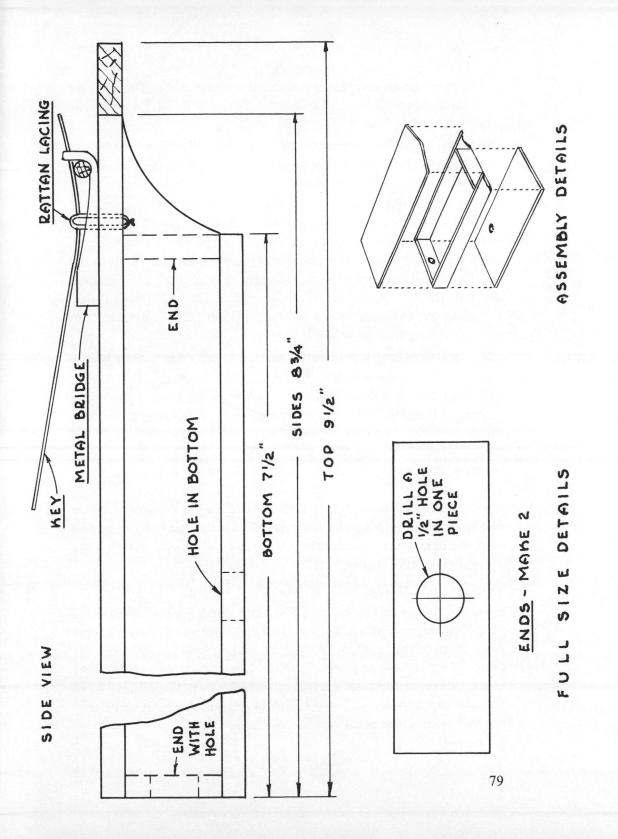

ROTTAN LACING

KEY

METAL BRIDGE

SIDE VIEW

END

END WITH HOLE

HOLE IN BOTTOM

BOTTOM 7½"

SIDES 8¾"

TOP 9½"

DRILL A ½" HOLE IN ONE PIECE

ENDS - MAKE 2

FULL SIZE DETAILS

ASSEMBLY DETAILS

79

bottom side of the top panel, thread the lace up through the second hole and down through the third hole and tie a knot on the underside.

10. Next, begin final assembly by positioning the metal bridge on the top, then place the anchor wire over it, dropping the ends in the two outer holes. The assembly is now ready for lacing.

11. Again, starting from the bottom side of the top panel, thread the rattan lace up through the second hole, over the top of the anchor wire, then back down through the same hole. Move to the third hole and lace it in the same manner. Continue lacing each hole until the twelfth hole is reached, drawing the lace taut as you go. Then loop the lace through the eleventh and twelfth holes and tie a knot on the underside the same as you did for the other end of the lace. Trim off excess length close to the knot.

12. Cut keys to length with wire cutters. Flatten ends slightly with a hammer. File ends smooth.

13. Place the wood dowel bridge in position at the ends of the metal bridge, then slip the keys, one at a time, over the metal bridge, under the anchor wire, and over the wood bridge. Sliding the keys forward or backward allows you to tune them. The two longest keys go in the center with progressively shorter keys placed on each side of them.

Note: For an additional tinkling effect, small ½″ square pieces of tin can stock rolled into tubular form around a ⅛″ metal rod can be slid over the keys during installation so that they lie loosely between the metal bridge and anchor wire.

TO USE YOUR THUMB PIANO:

Hold the instrument in both hands. Pluck the keys with the tips of your thumbs, one at a time, by pressing down on the ends of the keys, then releasing them sharply by sliding your thumbs off the ends. The tonal range of the instrument will vary with the quality and hardness of the steel keys. Keys may be tuned by sliding them forward or backward to lengthen or shorten them, resulting in raising or lowering the pitch.

SAGAT PLAYER FROM
UNITED ARAB REPUBLIC

This simple clown not only has a heritage of thousands of years, but is a link in the cultural chain spanning the ancient dynasties of Egypt and the Arab world of today.

The little man, dressed in typical Arab fashion, has been played with by children of Egypt since ancient times. The metal clappers in each hand represent a rhythm instrument, the *sagat*, or brass castanets, of the belly dancers—the dancers, however, hold two clappers in each hand.

The tasseled red cap, or *tarbush*, is a typically Egyptian headdress, and even those men who have adopted European dress still retain the custom of wearing a red tarbush.

The blue shirt represents the traditional blue cotton *jubbah*, a long cloth robe worn by the men.

The little man's head is made of chalk which is then dipped in wax as a preservative. This, too, is in keeping with the past—for, since ancient times, Egyptians have utilized the rich deposits of limestone along the banks of the River Nile.

To this day, in the rural areas of Egypt, the Sagat Player has retained its age-old popularity. It is seen most often during the 9th month of the Muslim lunar calendar—the month that the Muslim people believe God revealed his teachings to the last of their great Prophets—Mohammed. These Islamic teachings, the Bible of the Arab World, are known as the Koran; the month of Ramadan in which the Koran was revealed is set aside as a fasting month. During this period, all Muslims believing Mohammed to be the messenger of God are expected to fast daily from sunrise to sunset.

The Sagat Player is a traditional toy for children during the evening festivities which are held throughout the month of Ramadan.

MATERIALS:

Use basswood, pine, or balsa for the following: 1 pc. 1″ square x 2″ for the head block; 1 pc. ⅜″ x ½″ x 1¾″ for the hinge block; 1 pc. ¼″ x 1″ x 2″ for the front block; 1 pc. ¼″ x 1″ x 2¾″ for the rear block; 1 pc. ⅟₁₆″ x ¾″ x 6½″ for the back slat; 2 pcs. ⁵⁄₁₆″ square x 1¾″ for the arms; 2—1½″ diameter discs cut from tin can stock for the cymbals; 1 pc. ⅜″ x 2⅝″ steel strapping for the spring; paper clips or equivalent size soft iron wire for the staple and hinges; 4—½″-20 wire nails; crepe paper for the shirt, colored paper for the cape; white glue; red model paint.

HOW TO MAKE IT:

Note: The original toy had a head carved from chalk. You will find it easier to carve the head from wood. The working drawings show full size details of the framework and mechanism without the paper coverings. The artist's sketch shows the paper costume.

1. Make the hinge block. Locate and prick the wire nail centers on the bottom of the block with a sharp-pointed tool.

2. Make the back block and back slat. Glue the hinge block to the top of the back block, centering it, and with the nail centers pointing down. Then glue the back slat to the assembly.

3. Make the front block and wire staple. Push the staple into the top of the block. See drawing detail for location and clearance measurement.

4. Make the spring from steel strapping. Cut pointed ends. Press the ends into the front and rear blocks. Check with the side view drawing to see that parts line up correctly.

5. Make the wood arms. Cut the cymbals from tin can stock. Punch or drill a ⅟₁₆″ hole in the center of each, then form a slight dimple in each center using a ball-peen hammer with the work supported by a soft wood block. Attach the cymbals to the arms with ½″-20 wire nails. Cymbals should be mounted so they swing freely on the nails.

6. Using the drawing for a pattern, make the two wire hinges. Start with a 3″ length of wire, bend in two, then wrap around a #18 wire

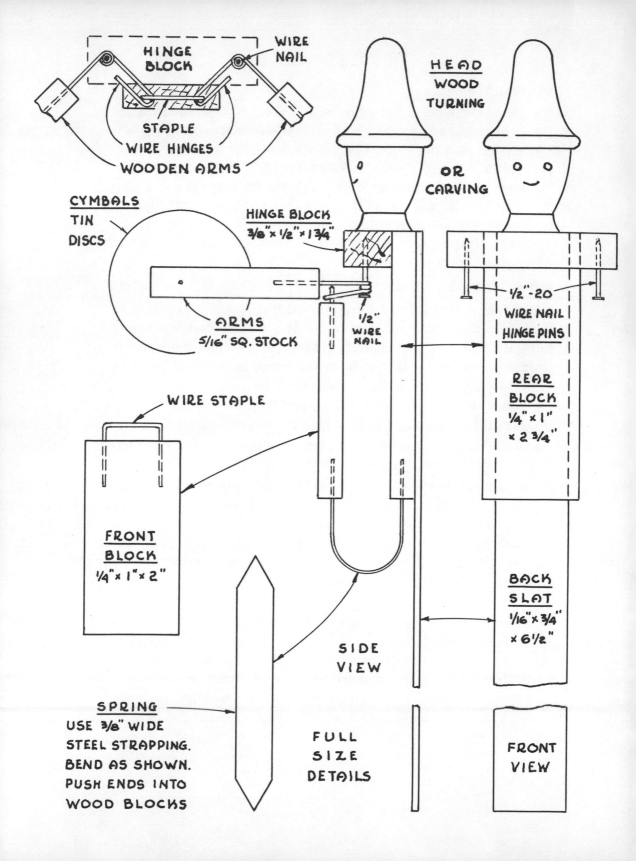

HINGE BLOCK — WIRE NAIL

STAPLE
WIRE HINGES
WOODEN ARMS

CYMBALS
TIN DISCS

ARMS
5/16" SQ. STOCK

HINGE BLOCK
3/8" × 1/2" × 1 3/4"

1/2" WIRE NAIL

HEAD WOOD TURNING

OR CARVING

1/2"-20 WIRE NAIL HINGE PINS

REAR BLOCK
1/4" × 1"
× 2 3/4"

WIRE STAPLE

FRONT BLOCK
1/4" × 1" × 2"

BACK SLAT
1/16" × 3/4"
× 6 1/2"

SIDE VIEW

SPRING
USE 3/8" WIDE
STEEL STRAPPING.
BEND AS SHOWN.
PUSH ENDS INTO
WOOD BLOCKS

FULL SIZE DETAILS

FRONT VIEW

nail twice leaving the ends finally extending at 90°. Drive the nail into a wood block to hold it steady during the bending operation. Bend the U on each hinge, trim ends to length, then press the straight portion into the end of the wood arm. Again, check with the drawing to see that the size of the hinges and arm location is correct.

7. Install the arms on the body by sliding each hinge loop around the staple, then press the ½"-20 wire nail hinge pin into the hinge block. Check operation of the mechanism by pressing the front block to see that arms swing freely and cymbals come together correctly.

8. Carve the head from a wood block. Glue it on top of the hinge block. Refer to drawing for correct position.

9. Make the shirt with a strip of crepe paper. Spot-glue to the front block and rear slat.

10. Make the cape by wrapping a piece of colored paper around the framework. Glue together on the back.

11. Paint the cap red. Mark the nose and eyes with pencil or paint.

TO USE YOUR SAGAT PLAYER:

Hold the clown between your thumb and fingers. Squeeze the front block with your thumb to make him crash the cymbals.

RUSSIAN BEAR FROM THE SOVIET UNION

Toward the end of the last Ice Age, some 20,000 years ago, Master Bear was regarded as the most holy of all wild animals. King of the Beasts, he roamed the northern hemisphere, making his home in natural caves across the Arctic from Finland and Russia to Siberia and Alaska; he wandered as far south as the foothills of the European Alps as well as over the northern parts of North America. He was looked upon as a god by our cave-dwelling ancestors, who centered many of their religious ceremonies around him.

Though the bear was not worshipped everywhere it was hunted, there is evidence that the bear cult was amazingly widespread. Even to this day, the festive ceremonies surrounding the sacrifice of the bear are still practiced in their prehistoric form by bear-hunting communities such as the Lapps in northern Russia and the Gilyaks of eastern Siberia. These people still look upon the bear as an immortal being who is not only of a higher order than man but who possesses greater intelligence and strength. His blood and flesh are said to have magical powers and those who feast upon him will acquire some of his strength. Furthermore, they believe that the bear can understand human speech, and refer to him by such secret names as "Master of the Forest," "Wise Man," or the "Old Man of the Mountain."

Though the number of persons worshipping the bear has dwindled greatly, the multinational population of the U.S.S.R. still have a special fondness for their "Honey-Paw." He is the central figure in many of their fairy tales: his head is a symbol of luck; a mythology has developed around him, and numerous superstitions are associated with his name. It is no wonder, therefore, that in the folk art of Russia, the figure of the bear has held a prominent place. In a land of forests, where woodcarvers artistically chisel scenes from daily life, the bear, who still roams freely in the sparsely populated woodlands of the North, is a favorite and traditional subject for craftsmen carving folk toys for Russian children.

MATERIALS:

1 pc. 1″ x 1⅛″ x 5¾″ basswood for the base block; 1 pc. ⅜″ x 1½″ x 1¾″ basswood for the basketball backboard; 1 pc. ⅞″ x 1¾″ x 3″ basswood for the animal body; 1 pc. ⅜″ x 1⅛″ x 2″ basswood for the arm yoke; 1 pc. ⅜″ x 4¾″ wood dowel for the post; 1 pc. 5/16″ x 3″ wood dowel for the plunger; 1 pc. 3/16″ x 13/16″ wood dowel for the plunger pin; 1—8″ length of fishline or fine string; 1—9/16″ diameter wood bead; 1—3¼″ length fine steel wire (paper clip size) for the basketball hoop; 1—5/16″ x 1¾″ fine steel wire compression spring (purchase at a hardware store or locksmith shop); 3—½″ #20 wire nails; white glue.

HOW TO MAKE IT:

1. Make the base first. Lay out the hole center in the top for the post hole, the hole center in the end for the plunger hole, and the position of the ¼″ x ⅞″ mortise as shown in the top view of the drawing.

2. Cut the mortise in the top of the block with a ¼″ chisel or a sharp modeler's knife—about ⅜″ deep. Then bore the ⅜″ holes for the post ½″ deep, the plunger 3¾″ deep. Finish the base by cleaning out the mortise and sanding smooth.

3. Draw a centerline around the sides of the animal block.

4. Now lay the block on its side over the animal drawing and mark the position of the 3/16″ dowel pin in the bottom of the block. At the same time locate the arm nail holes. Drill the 3/16″ dowel hole ¼″ deep, the arm nail holes with a #20 wire brad or common pin for a drill.

5. Sketch, or make a tracing of the animal outline and transfer the outline to the side of the body block with carbon paper. Saw or carve the body profile, then whittle or carve the animal following the artist's rendering for details of the right side and the working drawing for the left side.

6. Make the arm yoke next. Drill the brad holes before sawing the outline. Carve the yoke with a curved recess or pocket in the paws to hold the wood bead as indicated on the drawing.

7. Now make the plunger. Locate and drill the 3/16″ hole for the dowel

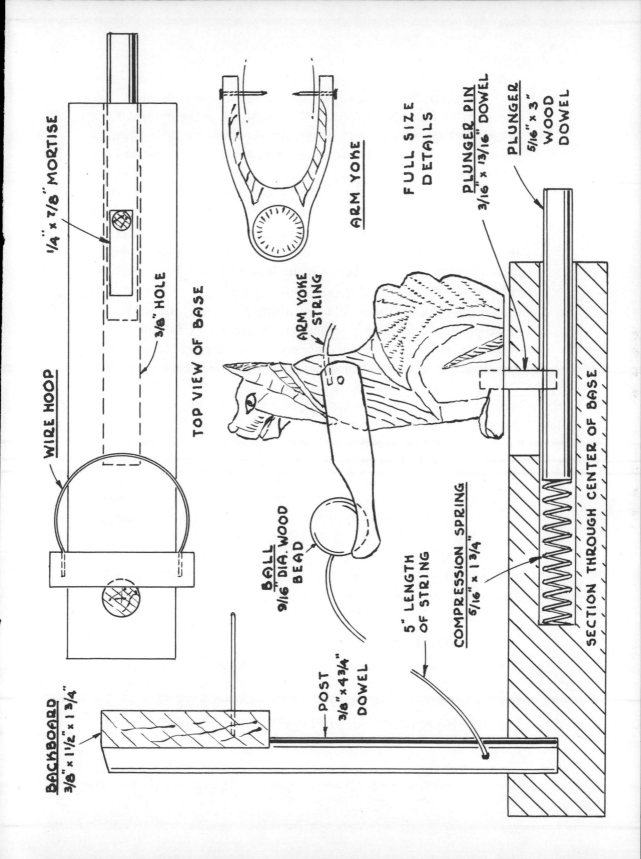

WIRE HOOP

1/4" x 7/8" MORTISE

3/8" HOLE

TOP VIEW OF BASE

ARM YOKE

FULL SIZE DETAILS

PLUNGER PIN
3/16" x 13/16" DOWEL

PLUNGER
5/16" x 3" WOOD DOWEL

ARM YOKE STRING

BALL
9/16" DIA. WOOD BEAD

COMPRESSION SPRING
5/16" x 1 3/4"

SECTION THROUGH CENTER OF BASE

5" LENGTH OF STRING

POST
3/8" x 4 3/4" DOWEL

BACKBOARD
3/8" x 1 1/2" x 1 3/4"

pin ³⁄₁₆″deep. Insert the compression spring in the base block followed by the plunger, then insert the dowel pin in the plunger for a test fit. Both the plunger and dowel pin should move freely without wobble. Glue the dowel pin in the plunger when the plunger and pin operate smoothly.

8. Install the arm yoke on the animal with a ½″ #20 wire nail on each side. Check to see that the arms move freely up and down.

9. Glue the animal in position on the plunger pin, allowing ¹⁄₁₆″clearance between the animal and the top of the base block. (Slip a notched piece of thick cardboard between the block and the base until the glue dries, then remove the cardboard.)

10. Drill a ¹⁄₁₆″hole about ¼″ deep in the right arm just above the hinge pin (see drawing); glue one end of a piece of fishline in this hole. After glue is dry, tie the other end of the line to a ½″ #20 wire nail driven into the base block as shown on the artist's rendering. The cord length should be just long enough so the arm yoke will hang slightly downward when the plunger is in the outer position and pull the arms up when the plunger is pushed all the way in.

11. Make the post, backboard, and wire loop as an assembly before installing it on the base block. File a flat on the post where contact is made with the backboard. Glue the backboard on the post. Clamp until glue is dry. Form the wire hoop, press ends into the backboard, then glue the post in the post hole in the base block. Line up the backboard so that it is square with the base block.

12. Drill a ¹⁄₁₆″hole near the base of the post about ¼″ deep. Glue one end of a 5″ length of cord in the hole, the other end in a similar hole in the wood bead.

13. The original toy was unpainted.

TO USE YOUR BASKETBALL PLAYER:

Place the wood bead in the arm yoke pocket. Push the plunger quickly to make the arms raise and throw the ball into the basket. It's not as easy to do as it looks! Take turns with a friend, each getting one shot at the basket for one turn. Make up a score system if you like.

90

PECKING BIRD FROM
POLAND—CZECHOSLOVAKIA

The historical events altering the boundary lines within Central and Eastern Europe have made it virtually impossible to pinpoint a specific country east of Germany as the creator of a particular folk toy. The pecking bird, in particular, is difficult to place, as the bird-shape has remained a favorite of woodcarvers since prehistoric times.

Pendulum-operated toys were certainly known as early as the third millenium B.C. and the bird-shape was a popular subject of woodcarvers during that era. Whether or not an actual pecking bird was made, however, is not known.

Birds with flapping wings and possibly even pecking beaks were played with by children of ancient Greece as well as by those of the Persian Empire. Their popularity continued in Mediterranean countries for almost 1500 years, until about A.D. 1000. Then, there was a 400-year span during which they were neither written about nor illustrated.

The records of the Middle Ages rarely make mention of children and their objects of play. There is no doubt that toys existed during this period, but they were not comparable to the elaborate toys of the ancient world. The children of medieval Europe were not afforded the luxury of play, as they were forced to work at the youngest possible age.

Even if their need for fun and relaxation had not been completely neglected, children in Germany and France, at the beginning of the 13th century, would have had no time to delight in the magic land of childhood. Filled with the crusading spirit of the times, they had banded together and were marching toward Jerusalem; they were determined to regain the Holy Land from the Turks. But the tragic sufferings of the Children's Crusade were short-lived. With the ending of this Crusade, adults directed much of their attention toward making the child's world a happy one, and toys regained their importance.

The modern pecking bird was certainly in vogue by the 15th century in central as well as northern Europe. Although it is being made today in many countries both as a folk art and as a manufactured toy, the handcarved Polish pecking bird and its relative from Czechoslovakia most closely resemble the 15th century, pendulum-operated bird that alternately pecked on a board and flapped its tail.

MATERIALS:

1 pc. 1″ square x 2¼″ basswood or pine for the body; 2 pcs. 3/16″ x 1″ x 2″ basswood, pine, or plywood for the head and tail; 1 pc. 3/16″ x 1″ x 8″ basswood or pine for the handle; 1 pc. 3/16″ x 1″ wood dowel for the supporting pin; 1 pc. ¾″ x 1″ x 1″ wood block for the weight, or substitute a large wooden spool; carpet or button thread; 2—¾″ #18 wire brads for hinge pins; white glue.

HOW TO MAKE IT:

1. Select a soft, straight-grained piece of wood for the bird body. Lay out the notches at both ends of the block and the dowel hole center in the bottom. Cut the notches and drill the 3/16″ dowel hole while the block is square. Locate and drill the hinge pin holes with a #18 wire brad.

2. Sketch, or use a pattern, to lay out the oval shape on the sides of the block, then carve, file, or sand the body to an egg-shape.

3. Trace the outlines of the head and tail, then transfer these outlines to the 3/16″ stock with carbon paper. Locate hinge pin holes at the same time.

4. Cut out head and tail pieces with a fine tooth blade in a coping saw or power jig saw. Clean up saw cuts with fine sandpaper. Drill 1/16″ holes for the hinge pins.

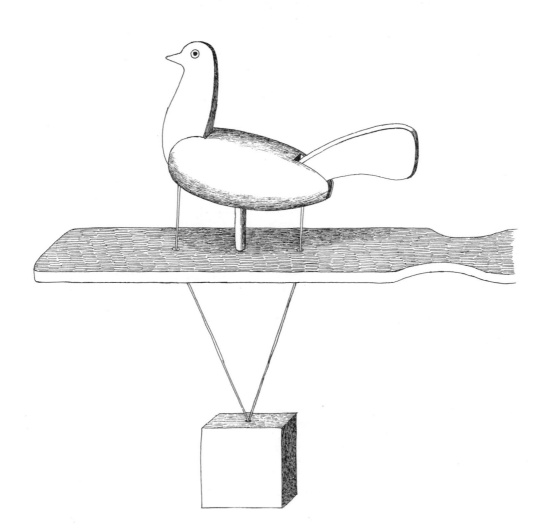

5. Draw the eye and bill lines on the head with a soft pencil.

6. Make the handle. Locate hole centers and drill the three ³⁄₁₆″ holes.

7. Tie one end of a 10″ length of carpet thread to the head by threading it through the hinge pin hole and tying a knot at the notch. Do the same with the tail. Check to see that both the head and tail slide freely in the body notches, then install the wire brad hinge pins. Double check both pieces for free movement up and down.

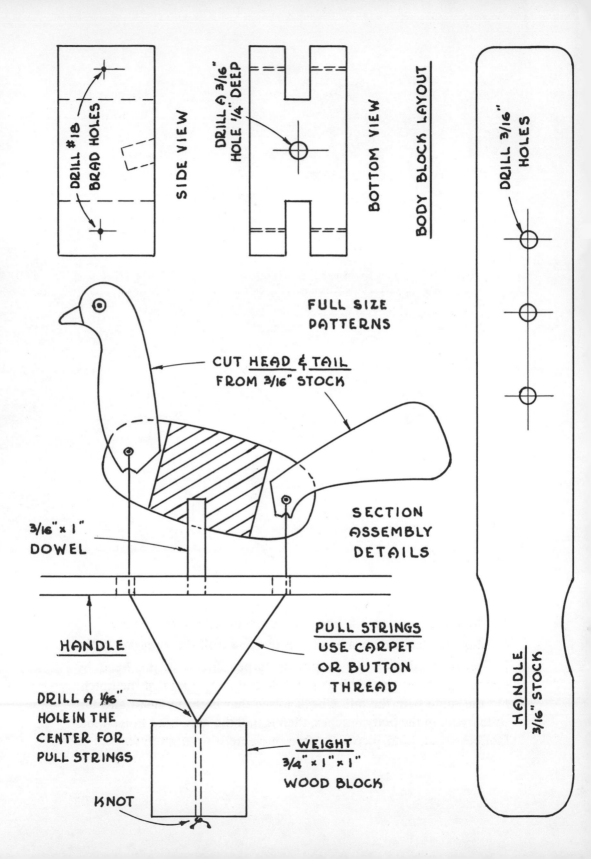

DRILL #18 BRAD HOLES

SIDE VIEW

DRILL A 3/16" HOLE 1/4" DEEP

BOTTOM VIEW

BODY BLOCK LAYOUT

FULL SIZE PATTERNS

CUT HEAD & TAIL FROM 3/16" STOCK

SECTION ASSEMBLY DETAILS

3/16" x 1" DOWEL

HANDLE

PULL STRINGS
USE CARPET OR BUTTON THREAD

DRILL A 1/16" HOLE IN THE CENTER FOR PULL STRINGS

WEIGHT
3/4" x 1" x 1" WOOD BLOCK

KNOT

DRILL 3/16" HOLES

HANDLE
3/16" STOCK

8. Glue the supporting dowel in the body block and the handle. Check with the drawing to see that spacing is correct. Line up the bird so it is straight with the centerline of the handle.

9. Make the weight block. Drill a $\frac{1}{16}''$ hole through the center.

10. Thread the pull strings through the first and third holes in the handle and tie them to the weight block, allowing the weight to hang two to three inches below the handle and centered under the bird.

Note: The original bird was left unpainted. You may paint yours if you like.

HOW TO OPERATE YOUR PECKING BIRD:

Hold the handle in one hand, then gently move the handle in a circle to activate the weight. Your bird should move his head and tail alternately to the ground as if eating.

WHERE TO GET MATERIALS

Due to space limitations, specific sources for the materials listed below cannot be given. However, typical sources of supplies are suggested so they may be obtained locally or through mail order houses. Addresses of local suppliers may be found in the "yellow pages" of any telephone book and mail order suppliers in hobby and craft magazines.

Pine, sugar pine, basswood, lattice stock—local lumberyards

Sheet and block balsa—hobby shops

Wood dowels—lumberyards and hardware stores

Nylon fishing line or builder's cord (chalk line)—hardware stores

Wire nails and brads—hardware stores

Copper wire, #12 and 14 gauge—scrap house-wiring cable—electrical supply houses

Bell wire—hardware, electrical supply, and radio parts stores

Curtain rings—department stores

Rattan—craft supply houses, chair seat repair shops

Leather and rawhide—leathercraft supply houses, shoe repair shops

Spring wire—locksmiths, clock shops, hardware stores

Iron wire—hardware stores, farm supply stores

Steel strapping—usually available as scrap at metal fabricators, plumbing shops, machine shops, or stores which sell electric appliances (used for strapping large boxes)

White glue, Duco-type cement—hardware stores, hobby shops

Tin can stock—use sides and ends of clean tin cans

Shellac and vinyl sealer—hardware stores

Model and acrylic paints—hobby shops, art supply stores

Strathmore Bristol board—art supply stores